LIVE AND LET OTHERS LIVE

MY MUSINGS

LESLIE M JOHN

LIVE AND LET OTHERS LIVE

MY MUSINGS

LESLIE M JOHN

DESCRIPTION

LIVE AND LET OTHERS LIVE

This book is the result of observing persecutions in India and other parts of the world, of Christians, and also mankind rising against mankind in various nations targeting innocent men, women and children. My deep feelings are for all those who suffered persecutions/deaths because of color, creed, ethnicity, race etc.

No offence is meant to any individual or any religion or any color, or any ethnicity.

White or black
Brown or of any other color
Our blood looks alike
Our images look alike

We are all God's creation
Out of dust we are made
And migrated to nations
Hatred and hurting are so bad

Seventy of eighty years we live
All our days we strive
And to the dust we return
No, no, do not shorten lives

Love neighbor as yourself
Love God with all your heart
Love God with all your soul
Live and let live in God's love

ABOUT THE AUTHOR

The author, who accepted Lord Jesus Christ as his personal Savior when he was a boy of 13, was raised in a Christian family and had education in Christian Institutions.

This then was the message that he heard of the Son of God, Lord Jesus Christ. This then is the message that he declares that God is light and in Him there is no darkness at all. Jesus Christ is the Son of God sent from above to save sinners.

Jesus died on the cross bearing our sins upon Himself. He was buried and God raised Him on the third day. Jesus, after having appeared to many for 40 days ascended to heaven. He will come again. Whosoever confesses his/her sins to Him and believe in heart that God raised Him from the dead will not perish but will have everlasting life.

"Jesus saith unto him, I am the way, the truth, and the life: no man cometh unto the Father, but by me" (John 14:6).

SCRIPTURES

Scriptures quoted in this book are from KJV from open domain, and from NIV, ESV, and NLT not greater than the number permitted.

ISBN-13: 978-0-9985181-6-9
ISBN-10: 0-9985181-6-6

Table of Contents

CHAPTER 1

TO THE UNKNOWN GOD

Epicureans and stoics, who debated with Paul about his preaching of Jesus Christ and Resurrection, treated him with contempt by calling him as "babbler". Some others accused him of proclaiming foreign gods. They took Paul and brought him to Areopagus (which is an earliest Government council run by the best individuals or a privileged class at Athens).

They demanded as to what and about whom Paul was preaching. They hardly understood what resurrection is all about, and who Paul was to teach about it. They accused him proclaiming of another king apart from Caesar. Resurrection was a new doctrine that was being forced into their ears. They demanded Paul speak at length of this new doctrine at Areopagus. Interestingly, Athenians of that period of time were very interested either to tell some stories of that thrill them, or hear some such stories. While Paul was speaking the knowledge of the truth, they considered such facts as myths.

By this time Paul had already seen in Athens that the city was fully given over to idols (cf. Acts 17:16). Athenians had several gods. One for each of their choice beliefs, emotions and creations. It is said that they had gods of every kind like, god of the arts, god of the carpenters, the god of the masons, the god of love, the god of peace, the god of war, the god of hate, the god of jealousy, the god of anger, etc. Paul also saw an altar with an inscription "TO THE UNKNOWN GOD". This was set up by Athenians with the notion that while worshipping several gods they might miss some god, whom they have not known and he might get angry on them.

Paul not only persuaded Epicureans, Stoics and God-fearing Gentiles but he seized the opportunity here at Areapagus. He, first appreciates them and their devotion, and then says to them that they were very religious.

"So Paul stood in the midst of the Areopagus and said, "Men of Athens, I observe that you are very religious in all respects" (Acts 17:22 NASB)

Then, Paul proceeds to delivers a wonderful sermon, commonly called "Sermon on Mars Hill" He continues preaching...

""For while I was passing through and examining the objects of your worship, I also found an altar with this inscription, 'TO AN UNKNOWN GOD.' Therefore what you worship in ignorance, this I proclaim to you. "The God who made the world and all things in it, since He is Lord of heaven and earth, does not dwell in temples made with hands; nor is He served by human hands, as though He needed anything, since He Himself gives to all people life and breath and all things; and He made from one man every nation of mankind to live on all the face of the earth, having determined their appointed times and the boundaries of their habitation, that they would seek God, if perhaps they might grope for Him and find Him, though He is not far from each one of us; for in Him we live and move and exist, as even some of your own poets have said, 'For we also are His children.' 29"Being then the children of God, we ought not to think that the Divine Nature is like gold or silver or stone, an image formed by the art and thought of man. 30"Therefore having overlooked the times of ignorance, God is now declaring to men that all people everywhere should repent, 31because He has fixed a day in which He will judge the world in righteousness through a Man whom He has appointed, having furnished proof to all men by raising Him from the dead." (Acts 17:23-31 NASB)

Does Paul's preaching teach Christians any lesson here? Paul presented the facts but did not condemn them nor antagonize them. In fact in cases where there was not much response to his peaching he departed from that place.

"Now when they heard of the resurrection of the dead, some began to sneer, but others said, "We shall hear you again concerning this." So Paul went out of their midst. But some men joined him and believed, among whom also were Dionysius the Areopagite and a woman named Damaris and others with them" (Acts 17:32-34 NASB)

When violence broke out at Jason's house...

"... the brethren immediately sent away Paul and Silas by night unto Berea: who coming thither went into the synagogue of the Jews" (Acts 17:10)

They were forcibly moved out of Berea...

"But when the Jews of Thessalonica had knowledge that the word of God was preached of Paul at Berea, they came thither also, and stirred up the people. And then immediately the brethren sent away Paul to go as it were to the sea: but Silas and Timotheus abode there still" (Acts 17:13-14)

"So Paul departed from among them" (Acts 17:33 KJV)

"But when divers were hardened, and believed not, but spoke evil of that way before the multitude, he departed from them, and separated the disciples, disputing daily in the school of one Tyrannus" (Acts 19:9)

Live and Let Others Live

CHAPTER 2

WHY I AM A CHRISTIAN? PART I

Christianity is not a religion, but it is a relationship with Eternal God. He is living God.

It is my belief that in the beginning there was the Word and the Word was with God and the Word was God and the Word became flesh and dwelt among us that recognizes me that I belong to the true God.

It is my belief that Lord Jesus Christ relinquished His glory that He had with the Father and incarnated in flesh and came down to this earth in the form of a servant and in the likeness of man.

I have acknowledged by my mouth that Jesus as my Lord and believed in my heart that God raised Him from the dead on the third day, and that is the reason why I am Christian.

I was born and raised in Christian family and was taught about Christianity from my childhood. It is my conviction that led me to believe that Jesus Christ is the true God and there is no salvation except by Him.

After having led as Christian for many years I was curious to know why I consider Christianity as the true relationship with God, and how Lord Jesus Christ so personal to me.

When I sought the Truth of the knowledge of God, in other religions they appeared to me so shallow that there is no hope for the future.

Apostle Paul asked the audience during the early days of proclamation of Gospel of Lord Jesus Christ as to why the rulers have laid great yoke on the people to believe that salvation is by not only faith but man has to contribute his part in securing salvation.

In other words, the efficacy of the blood of Lord Jesus Christ shed for the sins of men fell short of the requirement to provide salvation mankind which is not true. The substitutionary death of Lord Jesus Christ was a perfect sacrifice fulfilled in all respects and the requirements of Old Testament laws.

The proclamation of Gospel of Jesus Christ began in the first century after the resurrection of Lord Jesus Christ into heaven after appearing for forty days before many witnesses not only as recorded in the Holy Bible but also in the writings of the Jewish Historian Flavius Joseph[1].

"Now therefore why tempt ye God, to put a yoke upon the neck of the disciples, which neither our fathers nor we were able to bear?" (Acts 15:10)

Apostle Peter rose up in the council at Jerusalem to ask a question as to why a great burden was being laid on men to believe God that certain rituals need to be observed to receive salvation. This situation occurred when some obstructionists entered into Christianity and said mere faith in Jesus was not enough to be saved but circumcision was necessary.

It was a time in the first century AD when Gospel of Jesus Christ was being proclaimed with great vigor, first in Jerusalem, and then in Judea and Samaria, and then in the uttermost parts of the world.

Cont...Part II

[1] Flavius Joseph Antiques Book XVIII Chapter 3 Para 3
[1] Flavius Joseph Antiques Book XVIII Chapter 3 Para 3
[2] PMID: 15081504 [PubMed – indexed for MEDLINE]
[3] International Standard Bible Encyclopedia, Sheol, Hades, Hell
⍰

WHY I AM CHRISTIAN – PART II

There are no strings attached to it and we do not need to do any additional good work to receive salvation. He paid it all by His precious blood. It is not by silver or gold, or by visiting any holy shrine that we receive salvation but by accepting the fact that Jesus died and rose again on behalf of us.

Circumcision was mandatory for all the children of Israel and for those who decide to follow the God of Israelites.

The sect of the Pharisees who believed, saying, "That it was needful to circumcise them, and to command them to keep the law of Moses"; but after deliberations at Jerusalem council it was announced by the apostles who had revelations from God that circumcision is not required to receive salvation. (Acts 15:1-5)

Apostle Peter, Apostle Paul and other apostles decided to gather in a council at Jerusalem to consider the demand as to whether the condition of being circumcised is right or not.

Considering the teaching of Lord Jesus Christ they said that circumcision was not taught by Jesus, keeping Sabbath as mandatory is done away with. While speaking to Jews Jesus mentioned about circumcision and said it was in keeping with the requirements of Mosaic Law given to the nation of Israel to separate themselves from other nations. In spite of the freedom given to all believers in Christ to approach God without any restriction some Judaizers still insisted on circumcision for becoming the child of God.

Jesus was a Jew and according to Mosaic Law he was circumcised on the eighth day. Jesus pointed to Pharisees and Sadducees that in keeping the law they were breaking the law by circumcising on the Sabbath, which was rest day and no servile work was to be done on that day.

Jesus fulfilled the Law and paid the price on the cross for the transgressions of everyone. Anyone accepting Him as savior will receive salvation free of cost. It is a free gift with no strings attached to it. I am redeemed not by silver or gold but by the precious blood of Lord Jesus Christ shed upon the cross.

When Jesus made it so simple to have salvation free by confession why would I have to walk thousand or more steps on a hillock to reach God? Is it not that man is making his salvation tough by his own writings and beliefs? When Bible teaches that the heavens are throne of God and the earth is His footstool, why would I have to seek him in temples?

I would not like to climb a hill on South India or have a dip in a polluted river in North India to find a god. My God is so near to me and He is within me and my body is His temple. Gathering in Church set up to have fellowship with God and with one another is not equivalent to finding God in a temple. I follow the commandment of my God who demanded from me to worship Him in Spirit and in Truth.

I would not like to have unending cycles of re-incarnations by my "Karma" with no hope to achieve "Moksha" in any cycle. There is no such thing as re-incarnation in Christianity, and I am happy to know that I will be instantly with God when I die.

Achieving "Moksha" by doing good works is impossible for me; and I will not be able to do good works all the time avoiding any evil to anyone in my life-time. It is not possible simply because I am human and not divine. That is to say "Karma" leads me into having repeated and unending incarnations. Assurance that one day we will be like god or will become god by "Karma" is, then, impossibility.

Not considering angels on par with human beings, it is clear that human being is the supreme creature among all the creation, and if so, according to certain other beliefs, the number of human beings in all the cycles should be either be equal or less; but we see the population is increasing, which means the people in all the previous cycles were good, and did all the good works to be born is human beings, a belief which I cannot accept. Or, is that universe has undergone several cycles of creation within the span of my birth and my grandson's birth? It is beyond my imagination that such cycles of creation could have occurred within one hundred years.

I would rather chose the easy method of remission of my sins by believing in Lord Jesus Christ, who paid the price for my sins, and does not require my good works as precondition to be with Him forever and ever after my death.

When Jesus made it so simple not to have circumcision and yet be saved why would I have to have to circumcision. I would not like to give away the skin of any part of my body to belong to God if that was the requirement to belong to a god.

Jesus mentioned circumcision once, to illustrate a point, when talking with the Jews as written in John 7:19-24 that it was part of life as a Jew to keep Mosaic Law given to the nation of Israel to separate themselves from the nations.(Leviticus 12:3)

WHY I AM CHRISTIAN – PART III

Jesus was circumcised when he was 8 days old as was required by every faithful male and fulfilled the Law. (cf. Luke 2:21; Galatians 4:4; Genesis 17:10-12). It is because Jesus fulfilled the entire law on behalf of me and also because there is no difference between Jew and Gentiles the requirement of being circumcised is ended for me. (cf. Ephesians 3:6; Colossians 3:11; Galatians 3:28; Colossians 2:13&14)

Peter, therefore, asks why still people tempt God to put yoke, on the neck of His disciples. The stringent laws were given to Moses for children of Israel to identify that they belong to Israel and not to nations. Those stringent laws were violated by them several times, because it was hard to keep them.

Even if one could keep nine out of the Ten Commandments, the tenth one, which says covet not your neighbor's wife or property was very hard to keep. That does not mean Jesus has relaxed that provision or men are not required to keep that law, but the violation of such law is forgivable by God on confession.

The Law pointed to the transgression and never redeemed anyone from sin, but Jesus who became the sacrifice on behalf of us, paid it all.

"Now therefore why tempt ye God, to put a yoke upon the neck of the disciples, which neither our fathers nor we were able to bear?" (Acts 15:10)

God is Triune that is He is the Father, He is the Son, and He is the Holy Spirit. Lord Jesus Christ is not inferior to the Father; by the title he is called as the "Son of God". God exists in three forms; and they are co-equal, co-existent, and yet they are not three Gods but one God.

I would not want offer temple-worship, rituals and sacraments to please the divine beings called "devas" or "gods", purportedly existing in unseen worlds, to respond to my prayers. My Lord is omniscient who hears my prayers from any part of the world, or in any situation and from any location. It is that great access God the Father has given to me through His Son Lord Jesus Christ, who is the only mediator between God and man; to speak to Him just as any child would speak to its father.

I am so privileged to have Holy Spirit indwell me to guide me, convict me, and enlighten me instead of depending on a satguru (true teacher) to know the transcendent absolute, good conduct, purification, and introspection. I do not need to perform "Yoga" or sit in meditations for months or years for God to enlighten me. My meditations are understood by me, when Holy Spirit guides me, and He reveals the mysteries in the Scriptures instantly when I surrender to my Lord Jesus Christ.

When people ask questions as to why God did what He did they are perhaps asking their questions in ignorance that God is Almighty, and He created everything for His pleasure. God created everything in heavens and on the earth and in the seas, all creatures that walk on the earth or fly in the air, or creeps or crawls on the earth; and everything that is under the waters. He is Almighty. He created for His pleasure.

God created beautiful and wonderful creatures called angels, of which the chief was Lucifer, who was most beautiful, from whom no secret hid, full of wisdom and understanding, wiser than Daniel, and rich. He was in Eden the garden of God, and every precious stone was his covering, "the sardius, topaz, and the diamond, the beryl, the onyx, and the jasper, the sapphire, the emerald, and the carbuncle, and gold", but when he has set in his heart that he is a God, and he sits in the seat of God, in the midst of the seas, he became "Satan". The word "Satan" means "adversary" and he is the chief of evil spirits, the devil and great adversary of humanity (cf. Ezekiel 28:1-19; Isaiah 14:12-20)

"How art thou fallen from heaven, O Lucifer, son of the morning! how art thou cut down to the ground, which didst weaken the nations! For thou hast said in thine heart, I will ascend into heaven, I will exalt my throne above the stars of God: I will sit also upon the mount of the congregation, in the sides of the north: I will ascend above the heights of the clouds; I will be like the most High" (Isaiah 14:12-14)

"Therefore thus saith the Lord GOD; because thou hast set thine heart as the heart of God" (Ezekiel 28:6)

"Thou hast been in Eden the garden of God; every precious stone was thy covering, the sardius, topaz, and the diamond, the beryl, the onyx, and the jasper, the sapphire, the emerald, and the carbuncle, and gold: the workmanship of thy tabrets and of thy pipes was prepared in thee in the day that thou wast created" (Ezekiel 28:13)

It should be noted that God does not give His glory to anyone. He is jealous. Call Him partial, or whatever your human perception can think of Him, but the LORD will not compromise on giving away His glory to any one or any god.

Cont…Part IV

☐ WHY I AM CHRISTIAN- PART IV

God cast away Satan from His presence, and yet Satan has access to heaven. There will come a time when Satan will be cast away fully from heaven to the earth.

It was when Lucifer, the chief Angels rebelled against the Almighty God, that their choices of choosing their followers began. God will not interfere with your choice and neither will Satan be able to interfere with your choice if you choose to belong to God. If you choose to be on God's side you will be in heaven or else you will be in hell along with Satan to whom you would belong if you do not belong to God. It is either this way or that way and there is no mid-way.

Some work out percentage population in the world and ask as to why large numbers of people are heading towards hell and God, who knows this fact very well, why He created the world. God does not want anyone to go to hell; not even one soul. He wants every single soul to be with Him in eternity and have fellowship with everyone just as He had with Adam and Eve before they sinned.

God knows everything. Calculations such 82% belong to Satan, or 32% of 16% only belong to God, are according to human perception. One thing is sure that if 70% of people choose to be followers of Satan, well then God takes only 30% to heaven and will leave out 70% to their choice. Now, the question would then be is it possible for Satan to choose 70% to be his followers? No. God has chosen 100% to be His followers and wanted all to be with Him in eternity.

Large numbers of people yield to the temptations, worldly pleasures offered by Satan, and live as Satan wants them to live. They build mansions, accumulate billions in banks even those who are suffering from diabetes and would not be able to eat sumptuously. They know pretty well that they cannot carry one single pie to heaven, yet the greed for accumulation of wealth keeps increasing in them.

Alexander the great wanted to conquer the world, but it is believed that he suffered from malaria when he was 33 years of age and died[2]. That shows that the pleasures offered by Satan are purely transient, and temporary. That which lasts in our life is our inner self, the soul that goes to heaven. Bible asks a question what if a man earns whole world and loses his own soul.

God knew that which is going to happen to 100% of the people as to where they will be in eternity. He does not take pleasure in large percentage of people going to hell, and that is why He provided a way out for 100% of the people. A simple confession of sins to God and acknowledging by mouth that Jesus is the Lord and believe in heart that God raised Him from the dead on the third day will give salvation to the one who confesses.

Lord Jesus Christ, who was with the Father, relinquished His glory with the Father and came down in the form of a servant and in the likeness of man to this world, and He lived among us to see that 100% of the people go to heaven and live with Him. God sent His only Son, Jesus to reconcile man to Him.

It is very good to know about God and come to Him. It is very good to know as to what He did and to know how man rebelled against God. The rebellion was known to God, but He did not make robots to wield power over them not to rebel. He chose 100% of the people whom He created to be with Him in eternity, but alas! If large percentage chooses to be with Satan in the hell, well God is not at fault. Man reaps what he sows.

It is man's choice to spend in hell where there is gnashing of teeth and the fire never quenches. If large percentage choose to be in hell, well, God allows that. It is not the fault of God or God's intentions. However, we are not competent to ask God, why He did what He did, because we are not gods, but men, creatures.

Every creature will bow to Him, whether by willingness or unwillingness in the end. That God is Jehovah, and He is the only God. There is no other god beside Him. His Son is Lord Jesus Christ, and the mystery is that the Father and the Son and the Holy Spirit are one. They are Triune, not three Gods. I do not believe in mythologies, and fabrications of man's imaginations. Satan was quite successful in deceiving men into wrong beliefs and make his followers to persecute the children of God.

God is all powerful and Almighty. He knows everything beforehand. He created heavens, earth, and all the planets for His glory. He created man in His own image, i.e. in pure and perfect, not that God had a physical structure like man. God is a Spirit. Man did not have Holy Spirit when he was created. God gave man, (Adam), woman (Eve) to be his wife, and they lived in Garden of Eden, which God planted for them.

Cont…Part V⬜

WHY I AM CHRISTIAN – PART V

God gave them freedom to eat and live happily and replenish and subdue the earth. God gave them choice to decide what they should do. God said to them they may eat any fruit from the garden but not the fruit of the tree which gives him knowledge to know good and bad and another to live forever.

God knows everything beforehand.

God created everything for His pleasure because He is Almighty.

God did not create Robots. He created man with intelligence to choose all the good for him.

Man disobeyed God and transgressed God's command.

By eating the forbidden fruit they gained knowledge to know good and evil, but what happened? They were naked before, but they did not feel bad or shame. All that they knew by eating the forbidden fruit was that they were naked.

The question again is why God created anything at all even when He knew that they will transgress His command. Yes, but God also knew that there is a way to save them, and bring them back to Him. He knew beforehand that by the blood of His Son, Jesus He could save them and make them to live happily forever in heaven where there is no cry, no death, no disease, and no worry. That is the final stage and God knew that before. He has chosen us before the foundation of the world. That is why He created everything.

"According as he hath chosen us in him before the foundation of the world, that we should be holy and without blame before him in love" (Ephesians 1:4)

Reading through the sacred scriptures of other religions will reveal that no religion other than Christianity teaches salvation is by substitutionary of death of the Son of God, who paid penalty for the remission of sins of all mankind.

Some prefer to say that there is no such thing as sin, and some prefer to say that no one can provide oneself as a substitutionary sacrifice for other man. Thus while there is hopelessness in other religions my relationship with God provides me hope that my sins are forgiven by God, and I will be with Lord Jesus Christ forever ever. We know that we will die and yet we set alarm, why? We have hope that will rise again.

There is life after death. We will rise from our graves. Many religions teach that there is no life after death and man will incarnate again as cat, or rat, or crow. While everyone chooses the best in re-incarnations, I chose everlasting life to be in glorified body with my Lord and Savior Jesus Christ in eternity.

When God created Adam and Eve the creation of mankind was complete. God is not creating any new creation now. Adam had two sons. 1. Cain and 2. Abel. Cain killed Abel and Cain had offspring; but how? Obviously Adam had more children; but then was it sin to marry his sisters? No, it is not at that time. There are seven dispensations starting from creation to the destruction and creation of New Heavens and the new earth. It is all one cycle.

There are no cycles of creation, preservation and destruction in Christianity and that gives me abundant hope that I have only one cycle to complete; one life on this earth, one death and one resurrection. It then ends my misery on this earth living in this earthly tabernacle made of dust associated with sickness. There is that great hope that I have that I will live in glorious body forever and ever with Lord Jesus Christ.

It is by man's choice that he has one or more children. Sometimes, God held the womb of women barren such as Sarai, for some time and Hannah for some time; but God gave then children later on.

Abram was promised of a child, but his wife Sarai was hesitant and sent into Abram her hand maid, Hagar who bore Abram a son, who was named as Ishmael. God reiterated His promise to Abram and when Abram was one hundred years old and Sarai ninety they had another son, who was called Isaac, who was the promised child. Abram and Sarai were renamed as Abraham and Sarah. Isaac had one two sons, Esau and Jacob, out of which God by His sovereign will chose Jacob as blessed one over Esau. Jacob had twelve sons.

Look at that, the generations continued and wickedness increased in the world, and during Noah's period God wiped out every wicked person from the face of the earth, except Noah's family. To them were born children and the world population increased. It is not God who is sending people batch after batch into this world, but man's redemption is not complete.

Man transgressed and if in Noah's period everyone repented, perhaps redemption plan of God would have been complete, but they rebelled against God, and increased in population. God scattered them across nations and until today one hundred percent of people did not repent of their sins. It continued until Jesus came and became a sacrifice on behalf of man and died on the cross, and was buried and was raised on the third day. This is the simple message being sent out to people again and again but man has his own questions according to his understanding and keeps rebelling against God.

Cont…Part VI

WHY I AM CHRISTIAN – PART VI

The plan of redemption will come to an end at some point which is known to God alone, and then will the elements of the earth and in skies will be burnt and will be no more.

When man dies his soul will be with Lord Jesus Christ if he was saved, or otherwise, he will wait in the grave to be raised for judgment at the great white throne. When second thief prayed to Jesus while dying on the cross, Jesus said "Today you will be with me in Paradise".

It also needs a study of what "Sheol", "Hades", "Gehanna", "Tartarus" are.

Sheol is The Abode of the Dead. It is not a state of Unconsciousness It is not a state of having been removed from God's Jurisdiction It is cited in relation to immortality

"For thou wilt not leave my soul in hell; neither wilt thou suffer thine Holy One to see corruption" (Psalms 16:10)

"Because thou wilt not leave my soul in hell, neither wilt thou suffer thine Holy One to see corruption" (Acts 2:27)

"He seeing this before spake of the resurrection of Christ, that his soul was not left in hell, neither his flesh did see corruption" (Acts 2:31)

Hades is same as Sheol. The word "Sheol" is used in Old Testament and the word "Hades" is used in New Testament.

"And Jesus said unto him, Verily I say unto thee, To day shalt thou be with me in paradise" (Luke 23:43)

"GEHENNA" This is Greek word which is translated as "Hell" in Matthew 5:22, 29; 10:28 etc., and refers one being in danger of hell fire.

"But I say unto you, That whosoever is angry with his brother without a cause shall be in danger of the judgment: and whosoever shall say to his brother, Raca, shall be in danger of the council: but whosoever shall say, Thou fool, shall be in danger of hell fire" (Matthew 5:22)

"Tartarus" is the place where the angels that sinned and cast down to hell are bound by "chains of darkness" (utter darkness) reserved unto judgment. They are the ones who did not keep their first estate but left their own habitation.

"For if God spared not the angels that sinned, but cast them down to hell, and delivered them into chains of darkness, to be reserved unto judgment" (2 Peter 2:4)

"And the angels which kept not their first estate, but left their own habitation, he hath reserved in everlasting chains under darkness unto the judgment of the great day". (Jude 1:6)

Let us think of a King of a country, who has an enemy who ventures fight with the former and attacks to seize his kingdom. Would not the king kill the soldiers of his enemy? Yes, is it not? He does it to protect his kingdom. It is not cruelty but self-defense. Our Country also has enemy and it fights enemy. Similar is the case with God, when Satan came and spread wickedness in the world, God destroyed the world with deluge.

There should be strong base or supporting material to substantiate before one asks questions like why God was unhappy prior to creation. Neither Bible or any secular book or any philosopher said that God was unhappy prior to creation. Why should one form an idea that God was not happy prior to creation? Why should one think that God is creating new animals, or plants, galaxy, Milky Way, seas, etc.?

Creation is complete in six days and seventh day God rested. After that there was no creation and no new plants or animals created. There is nothing God is creating now endlessly. God is eternal and He lives outside man's time. Creation is explained in Genesis Chapter 1 and very important events are recorded in Genesis Chapter 2 and 3.

Cont…Part VII

WHY I AM CHRISTIAN – PART VII

Few verses from Genesis Chapter 1 are quoted below:

"Then God said, 'Let us make man in our image, after our likeness. And let them have dominion over the fish of the sea and over the birds of the heavens and over the livestock and over all the earth and over every creeping thing that creeps on the earth.' " "So God created man in his own image, in the image of God he created him; male and female he created them" "And God blessed them.

And God said to them, 'Be fruitful and multiply and fill the earth and subdue it, and have dominion over the fish of the sea and over the birds of the heavens and over every living thing that moves on the earth.' And God said, "Behold, I have given you every plant yielding seed that is on the face of all the earth, and every tree with seed in its fruit. You shall have them for food. And to every beast of the earth and to every bird of the heavens and to everything that creeps on the earth, everything that has the breath of life, I have given every green plant for food." And it was so. And God saw everything that he had made, and behold, it was very good. And there was evening and there was morning, the sixth day"

Few verses from Genesis Chapter 2 are quoted below:

"Thus the heavens and the earth were finished, and all the host of them. And on the seventh day God finished his work that he had done, and he rested on the seventh day from all his work that he had done. So God blessed the seventh day and made it holy, because on it God rested from all his work that he had done in creation" (Genesis 2:1-3 ESV)

God is a Spirit: and they that worship him must worship him in spirit and in truth. (John 4:24)

God created everything for His pleasure. We do not know what He was before Genesis 1. All that we know is that "In the beginning, God created the heavens and the earth. The earth was without form and void, and darkness was over the face of the deep. And the Spirit of God was hovering over the face of the waters".

Why He created what He created is not within my purview to peruse and I cannot question God as to why He did what He did.

There is no new creation after what He created that which is created as written in Genesis Chapter 1. There will be New Creation – New heavens and the New Earth.

This is what God says:

For, behold, I create new heavens and a new earth: and the former shall not be remembered, nor come into mind. (Isaiah 65:17)

God will destroy the present creation.

"But the day of the Lord will come as a thief in the night; in the which the heavens shall pass away with a great noise, and the elements shall melt with fervent heat, the earth also and the works that are therein shall be burned up" (2 Peter 3:10)

God did not say one should not question to know the facts. Usually, we notice two parts in one's questions. The quest to know is quite good. It shows that one is coming nearer to God. The second part of the questioning is merely the authority of God which is bad.

If I cannot question what one's is doing in his capacity within the powers one has how can I question the sovereign God of His authority? If I ask you a personal question it may account as intruding into one's privacy and one can say one should not such questions. Similarly, God does not want us to ask Him of His authority.

God created man in His own image. He, in His authority tested God whether man will be obedient or not. Man failed. Then, God tried in many ways to see whether man becomes obedient to Him. There seven periods of time called the seven dispensations. First, God dealt with man individually. Man rebelled; that is man failed to obey God. Then, there are six more dispensations and it is all in one cycle.

When wickedness increased on the face of the earth God destroyed man by flood but saved Noah and family who were righteous. When God saw that man is only a dust he decided not to destroy mankind any more with the flood and set a bow in the sky and made covenant with Noah that He will not destroy mankind any more by the flood.

God made covenant with Abraham, and that was unconditional. Genesis Chapters 12 to 15 have the details of Abrahamic Covenant. That covenant had seven distinct parts, a study that requires connecting Apostle Paul's writings in Galatians.

Paul, by the revelation of God, wrote in Chapters 3 and 4 of Galatians that Law was a school master. Heir cannot inherit when he is child. It is like a child until he reaches certain age he cannot write a check. Law was our school master and when the fullness of the time was come, that is when the time to offer sacrifices was over, God sent His Son Jesus Christ, who came under the law, and He fulfilled the Law.

According to prophesy in the book of Isaiah Chapter 53 Jesus died on the cross and was buried. He was raised by the God the Father on the third day. He was seen by many people when He was on this earth for forty days after His resurrection, and then He ascended into heaven. Now He is seated on the right hand of the Majesty, pleading on your behalf. All our sins, no matter how serious they are, will be forgiven by God, when we confess our sins to Jesus, and accept Him as Lord, and believe in heart that God raised Him from the dead. (Read Romans 10:9)

These are not fables but true happenings. There are no loop-holes in Christianity. There are no books in any religion, where you will find a savior who gave His life for our sake and who can forgive our sins in order to save us from perishing eternally. Christianity is not without any hope of un-ending re-incarnations.

Cont....Part VIII

WHY I AM CHRISTIAN – PART VIII

SIN AND RIGHTEOUSNESS

When I was at an Automobile center for an oil change the Automobile mechanic who was attending on my car engaged me in a small talk on religion and suggested casually to me that I should convert to his religion. His appeal was genuine and the thought was pestering my mind for quite long. Consequently, I thought of comparing my faith in Christ to that of his faith, primarily to discover what is better in his religion that surpasses mine that I should change my mind.

SIN

It all started out to be good and for the most part initially that I did not find much of difference; however as I perused more into the beliefs of adherents of his religion, I discovered that many of their beliefs differ from that of mine. His religion, which is a religion of 'submission', did not promise me better ways to receive everlasting life than that of my relationship with Lord Jesus and His teachings that captured me.

The view of the adherent of the religion of "submission" is that man is considered as having committed sin when he violates the God's commandments. According to them God created human with a clot of blood and the spirit in human is created with fire. They do not believe in the original sin that Christians believe in; but believe that in spite of Adam and Eve begging for pardon of their sin, God forgave them of their sins but punished them to live mortal life until the Last day when He will remove them from the earth and make them like gods.

They say just as the first pair was forgiven of their sins, true repentance will bring salvation to sinners. It is the pride that is considered as the primary sin and the primary virtue is submission. They do not believe in sin being passed onto to next generation. They often quote Deuteronomy 24:16, Ezekiel 18:20 from the Bible to disprove that original sin cannot be passed onto offspring.

Bible says: "The fathers shall not be put to death for the children, neither shall the children be put to death for the fathers: every man shall be put to death for his own sin" (Deuteronomy 24:16)

"The soul that sinneth, it shall die. The son shall not bear the iniquity of the father, neither shall the father bear the iniquity of the son: the righteousness of the righteous shall be upon him, and the wickedness of the wicked shall be upon him" (Ezekiel 18:20)

In fact these verses are misquoted and misunderstood to prove non-existence of original sin. The rules in Deuteronomy 24:16 were given for the guiding the Judges to help them decide cases where crimes are committed. In such cases where it becomes necessary to decide whether the children or fathers of those who commit crimes should be held responsible, it is obvious that neither parents nor children can be held responsible because the crime of one cannot be attributed to others. The person committing crime should bear the consequence. This is different from God's Law. There is no point in arguing from human point of view and comparing secular law with God's Law.

When it comes to deal with the Law of God, the transgressor of the command of the God, is not only held responsible for the crime he/she has committed against

God, but his/her offspring as well. It is God's law; that which cannot be overwritten by any one of us.

Adam and Eve represented not only themselves as humans, but they represented whole humanity. By one man's transgression the sin permeated into his offspring, because he was the representative of whole humanity.

Here is their confusion. They say God cannot have Son and God cannot be called either as "Son of God" or "Son of man". For the one who believes in Biblical evidences there are many verses to show that God is Triune; three in One. They are not three Gods, neither is anyone of them is inferior to the other. They exist as one, yet they had and have different roles to perform. None of them is separable one from the other.

Cont.…Part IX

WHY I AM CHRISTIAN – PART – IX

LORD JESUS EXPLAINS OF HIMSELF

Pharisees and Sadducees accused Him of His father was Joseph and Lord Jesus gave them an apt reply.

"Then said they unto him, Where is thy Father? Jesus answered, Ye neither know me, nor my Father: if ye had known me, ye should have known my Father also" (John 8:19)

"I said therefore unto you, that ye shall die in your sins: for if ye believe not that I am he, ye shall die in your sins" (John 8:24)

"So they said to him, 'Who are you?' Jesus said to them, 'Just what I have been telling you from the beginning. I have much to say about you and much to judge, but he who sent me is true, and I declare to the world what I have heard from him.'

They did not understand that he had been speaking to them about the Father. So Jesus said to them, 'When you have lifted up the Son of Man, then you will know that I am he, and that I do nothing on my own authority, but speak just as the Father taught me. And he who sent me is with me. He has not left me alone, for I always do the things that are pleasing to him." As he was saying these things, many believed in him'" (John 8:25-32 ESV)

THE TRUTH SHALL SET YOU FREE

"So Jesus said to the Jews who had believed him, 'If you abide in my word, you are truly my disciples, and you will know the truth, and the truth will set you free.'" (John 8:31-32 ESV)

The title "Son of man" has come from the prophecy in Daniel 7:13 wherein Daniel saw vision of the Messiah in human form.

"I saw in the night visions, and, behold, one like the Son of man came with the clouds of heaven, and came to the Ancient of days, and they brought him near before him" (Daniel 7:13)

Lord Jesus is the "Son of God" because He came from heaven and He was the only begotten Son of the Father. He was with God and He was God. He is divine. He was born as man to Virgin Mary "for that which is conceived in her is from the Holy Spirit".

Lord Jesus said about Himself as…

"For even the Son of man came not to be ministered unto, but to minister, and to give his life a ransom for many" (Mark 10:45)

Lord Jesus was born of the Virgin Mary, and ignorance or deliberate feigning of ignorance of the facts about His birth is the reason for such error. Here is the passage of the birth of Lord Jesus Christ.

"Now the birth of Jesus Christ took place in this way. When his mother Mary had been betrothed to Joseph, before they came together she was found to be with child from the Holy Spirit. And her husband Joseph, being a just man and unwilling to put her to shame, resolved to divorce her quietly. But as he considered these things, behold, an angel of the Lord appeared to him in a dream, saying, 'Joseph, son of David, do not fear to take Mary as your wife, for that which is conceived in her is from the Holy Spirit. She will bear a son, and you shall call his name Jesus, for he will save his people from their sins.' All this took place to fulfill what the Lord had spoken by the prophet: 'Behold, the virgin shall conceive and bear a son, and they shall call his name Immanuel' (which means, God with us). When Joseph woke from sleep, he did as the angel of the Lord commanded him: he took his wife, but knew her not until she had given birth to a son. And he called his name Jesus" (Matthew 1:18-25 ESV).

The prophecy in Isaiah 9:6 was fulfilled here.

"For to us a child is born, to us a son is given; and the government shall be upon his shoulder, and his name shall be called Wonderful Counselor, Mighty God, Everlasting Father, Prince of Peace. (Isaiah 9:6 ESV)

Apostle Paul explains about Lord Jesus as follows:

"Who, being in the form of God, thought it not robbery to be equal with God: But made himself of no reputation, and took upon him the form of a servant, and was made in the likeness of men: And being found in fashion as a man, he humbled himself, and became obedient unto death, even the death of the cross. Wherefore God also hath highly exalted him, and given him a name which is above every name" (Philippians 2:6-9)

Therefore, the atonement of sins of mankind provided by Lord Jesus Christ, once and for all, was substitutionary on behalf of men, just as bullocks and goats were offered as sacrifices during the Old Testament period, year after year. By one man's death the propitiation of sins of mankind was rendered. The 16th Chapter of book of Leviticus has details as to how the two goats (one of Lord and the other "scape goat" become the vital sacrifice on behalf of men).

Lord Jesus Christ fulfilled this criterion, once and for all, bearing our sin upon Himself. He, who knew no sin, became sin for us and died on the cross on behalf of us. He is the High Priest after the order of Melchizedek.

"For as by one man's disobedience many were made sinners, so by the obedience of one shall many be made righteous" (Romans 5:19)

He is God, and He is the 'everlasting Father" (cf. Isaiah 9:6), who relinquished His glory with the Father and came down into this world to become propitiation for us. He said He and the Father are one.

The essence of the law was rightly executed by one of the Kings of Judah by name Amaziah, who killed those who killed his father, but did not kill their children in order to comply with the provisions of the law in Deuteronomy 24:16. That is to say Amaziah did not do any harm nor did he hold the children of murderers guilty for killing his father.

"But the children of the murderers he slew not: according unto that which is written in the book of the law of Moses, wherein the LORD commanded, saying, The fathers shall not be put to death for the children, nor the children be put to death for the fathers; but every man shall be put to death for his own sin" (2 Kings 14:6)

True, it is the pride and rebellion that played vital role in the beginning. It is the pride of Lucifer that resulted in him becoming Satan and it is the rebellion of man and woman in the Garden of Eden that resulted in them being thrown out from the Garden of Eden.

However, in the light of the attempts made to prove that there is no original sin based on the verses quoted above are wrong. The original sin of Adam and Eve transgressing the LORD's commandment was not against men, but it was against God, and therefore, it passed onto generations after them as well.

It is the transgression of God's commandment and not man's that passed on to their descendants and such transgression required reconciliation. Everyone needs to confess one's sin and father cannot confess the sins of his children nor can the children confess the sins of their fathers.

That is why I consider Christian belief that Adam's sin is inherited by everyone on the earth, and all have come short of the glory of God, is the right belief. Reconciliation is possible only by the blood sacrifice and it was provided by none other than Lord Jesus, who paid the price on the cross.

There is another religion, a religion of "Dharma" and "Karma" which teaches me that there is nothing like "sin" but only "Karma" and our future depends on our "Karma". As for "Dharma" it is the belief that creation needs to be upheld and sustained in its place by following its laws in order that it may not fall apart. It is similar to a picture where a god holds a globe in his hands in order that it may not fall apart.

"Dharma" hopefully prevents such falling apart and contributes to avoiding degrading ourselves, and helping all-round progress, when we obey the laws of the universe.

The message of the Bible is not of religion but of relationship with God. Firstly, it is the relationship with God, which we may call it as a vertical relationship, and secondly, it is relationship with neighbor, which we may call it as horizontal relationship.

In the New Testament Lord Jesus condensed all the Ten Commandments into two by saying "Love the LORD with all your soul, with all your heart, with all your soul and with all your mind", which is the first commandment, and the second is to love your neighbor as yourself".

"Jesus said unto him, Thou shalt love the Lord thy God with all thy heart, and with all thy soul, and with all thy mind. This is the first and great commandment. And the second is like unto it, Thou shalt love thy neighbour as thyself. On these two commandments hang all the law and the prophets". (Matthew 22:37-40)

It is clear that every human being is depraved and the so-called 'righteousness' of human beings is like filthy rags. It is only by the grace of God that one is saved, and that message sounds good to me.

I see great concern that the religion that says they teach peace obviously does not practice what they teach. Going by the reports and video evidences of persecuting Christians it is hardly believable that those who commit such grave atrocities are true adherents of the religion of "submission".

RIGHTEOUSNESS

Whereas my faith in Christ teaches that good works are the result of having received salvation and such good words follow the salvation but not precede the essence of salvation most other religions teach differs one from the other. One speaks of "Moksha" after several re-incarnations and the other speaks of good deeds as pre-condition to procure a place in heaven.

I had already problems with "Karma" that possibly leads to "Moksha" by doing good works during my entire life-period. I would not be able to comply with this requirement which probably ends up in my having several re-incarnations such as crow, or eagle, or rat before I receive "Moksha". After several re-incarnations I would also perhaps lose a place in heaven according to the tenets of those religions who preach "Moksha" or heaven by doing good deeds.

As I pondered over this problem I was wondering how well my good works should be for God to love me. Bible says my righteousness is like filthy rags, and if so how could I escape from the wrath of God if I go by the standards of Lord Jesus, who said if I lust after a woman it is equivalent to having already committed adultery with her, and if I call my brother "fool" I am in danger of being thrown into hell-fire?

Speaking of good works there is provision of entering into the kingdom of God by doing good works, but that stage is in the final phase on this earth when Jews suffer during the Great Tribulation period. That time is not yet ripe; then my question would again be as to how would all the previous generations before me have entered the Kingdom of God, if it was not for the offering of sacrifices of animals on the altar, and high priest entering into the Holy of Holies once a year, and sprinkling the blood of sacrificed animals on the "Mercy seat" followed by his coming out of the Tabernacle and confessing the sins of the congregation on the head of 'scapegoat', which would then be released into the wilderness carrying the sins of the people never to return again. Good news is that Lord Jesus Christ paid price on behalf of everyone, whether of previous generations, or of this generation or of future generations. All that one needs is to believe in Jesus Christ, who made a way for our redemption from sin by His death on the cross, His burial and resurrection.

I was in pursuit of finding a sure and precise explanation of what it means to do good works and how good my works should be to receive salvation. I have questioned myself as to how would adherents of other religions do such good works as to make them eligible to secure a place in heaven? Their beliefs are not on par with my beliefs; and if they are no better than that of mine, there is no reason why I should consider their beliefs as right.

Cont.…Part X

WHY I AM CHRISTIAN – PART X

THE FIVE PILLARS AS I SEE

1. I confessed that my God is the true God and He is love. God sent His only Son into this world to die for my sins that by believing in Him I will not perish but have everlasting life. The Father and The Son are one, as the Son Himself said it so. I do remember this every day.

2. There were days in the Old Testament when the children of Israel were under captivity in Babylon. It was then Daniel opened the window of his chamber that faced towards Jerusalem and prayed three times a day and God heard his prayer.

It had connotation to King Solomon's prayer to God if the children of Israel prayed facing Jerusalem their prayers may be answered. God answered such prayers and provided ways for all the willing children of Israel to return in three phases to Israel during Ezra and Nehemiah's period.

Such contingency of saying prayers facing in one direction is redundant now inasmuch as the veil in the temple was rent into two from top to bottom when Lord Jesus was crucified on the cross. If rending of the veil from top to bottom was by God, then it surely opened the way for Gentiles and Jews to approach God without any formal methods or mediators, as was being done in the Old Testament period.

By offering Himself as a sacrifice on the cross Lord Jesus became the only mediator between God and men, thus providing free access to the Almighty God through Him.

3. When alms are given physically the hand of the giver is always above that that of the recipient's, and therefore, and for many other reasons giving is better than receiving. God blesses them that give to the poor but that, I believe, cannot be taken as one of the criterion to enter into heaven.

The question would then be can everyone give as much as required by God lest there should be different types of blessings in heaven for people with different amounts of alms they give. Bible does not prescribe alms-giving as a pre-condition to secure a place in heaven. It is the grace of God that is needed, and such grace comes by faith in Lord Jesus Christ, who paid the price in full with His precious blood.

4. I seldom fast on Good Friday or any other day deliberately to receive any favors from God because I know my God does not accept bribe to bless me. He blesses me according to the thoughts that I have in my heart. He is known as the one who searches the hearts. I would not like to think of getting into heaven by fasting on any festival simply because Bible never prescribed any such condition and, therefore, fasting does not meet the convictions of my heart.

5. If only pilgrimage to Holy Shrine could provide me a place in heaven I could do so; but the question is how many in the world are privileged to bear the costs of travel and accommodation? I for one, did not have the privilege of visiting Jerusalem until now, and what if I die now? There may be a very small percentage of people who visit Holy Shrines to meet such criterion, and it is very true that large percentage of people would not be able to do that in their life time. It, therefore, leaves behind a question as to whether God would consider it as a righteous act or

prescribe such condition for us to secure a place in heaven; obviously not! Thank God I am safe and sure of entering heaven.

In Titus Chapter 3:1-7 the Scriptures admonish us to be submissive to rulers and authorities, to be obedient, to speak no evil, to avoid quarrelling, to be gentle, to show perfect courtesy toward all people.

No doubt all these are good works but they do not bring salvation to us. Our soul to be free from sin and to inherit heavenly blessings there is much more to be done, and that is to accept the goodness that God has done for us.

The Lord saves us not because of our righteousness, but according to His mercy, by the washing of regeneration and renewal of the Holy Spirit. God poured out on us Holy Spirit richly through Jesus Christ our Savior. Believing Jesus as the Lord is the only criterion to be justified by His grace, in order for us to become heirs according to the hope of eternal life.

"Remind them to be submissive to rulers and authorities, to be obedient, to be ready for every good work, to speak evil of no one, to avoid quarreling, to be gentle, and to show perfect courtesy toward all people. For we ourselves were once foolish, disobedient, led astray, slaves to various passions and pleasures, passing our days in malice and envy, hated by others and hating one another. But when the goodness and loving kindness of God our Savior appeared, he saved us, not because of works done by us in righteousness, but according to his own mercy, by the washing of regeneration and renewal of the Holy Spirit, whom he poured out on us richly through Jesus Christ our Savior, so that being justified by his grace we might become heirs according to the hope of eternal life" (Titus 3:1-7 ESV)

Again, the insistence of the Automobile mechanic came to my remembrance and I thought of meditating on after-life according to his beliefs. There is much resemblance of the beliefs of adherents of his beliefs and mine but here is the crux of the problem.

According to the beliefs of the adherents of his religion all souls will be resurrected in their physical bodies on the Last day and stand before God and they will be judged according to the good and bad deeds that they did in their life before their death. They enter into Paradise if they did good deeds and enjoy physical and spiritual blessings forever or else they will be judged for their bad deeds that they did while they were on this earth. After the judgment is over, they will be thrown into hell to suffer physical and spiritual torment forever. The ordeal of facing final judgment is like walking over a narrow bridge from where one slips into hell if one did bad deeds in his physical life before death or does not slip but walks across the narrow bridge successfully to the other side to enter into Paradise.

There are two exceptions to this judgment and they are (1) if the warriors fought the cause of God they are caught up into the presence of God immediately (2) Enemies of "submission" to God are sentenced to Hell upon their death.

I am not sure what those good works are which make men become warriors for God and what those bad works are which make men enemies of God. There seems to be a contradiction in the beliefs of religion of "submission" in terms of the torment that the enemies face in hell-fire.

The first category remain as dead until the last day to be resurrected in their physical bodies with their souls to be judged; and the second category of people are sentenced to Hell upon their death without waiting for the Last day.

The first category of people has a strange way of being judged. They walk on the narrow bridge over the hell, and they slip automatically because they did bad deeds in their lives. Another category of people, who are enemies of God, are instantly judged when they die and be cast into the hell-fire and are tormented there. The distinguishing factor in the punishment that they receive here is the time-gap.

The first category of people wait until the last day, and the second category of people are instantly called, after their death, to be cast into the hell-fire. It does not make any sense, because the dead soul remaining in the grave does not know how long he/she waited in the grave before he/she is cast into hell-fire. The duration is infinite and same for both the categories, of course!

As mentioned before, the Bible says by one man's transgression we all have become enemies of God and it is only by the grace of God that we can have salvation. The first resurrection is not for unbelievers but is for believers in Christ, who resurrect to be with the Lord forever and ever. All unrepentant sinners will be condemned to be cast into the "lake of fire". It is very clear in the Bible that those who die in their sins will be resurrected and it is the "Second Resurrection" and their life in the "lake of fire" is the second death.

I, therefore, did not find any good reason to believe that beliefs of other religions are better than my relationship with God. I stick on to my beliefs.

WHY I AM CHRISTIAN – PART XI

SUFFERINGS AND RESTORATION

"And after you have suffered a little while, the God of all grace, who has called you to his eternal glory in Christ, will himself restore, confirm, strengthen, and establish you" (1 Peter 5:10 ESV)

For a believer in Christ sufferings are part of life and he/she rejoices in "…knowing that suffering produces endurance, and endurance produces character, and character produces hope, and hope does not put us to shame, because God's love has been poured into our hearts through the Holy Spirit who has been given to us" (Romans 5:3-5 ESV)

There is great hope that after we suffer a little while God will restore us, confirms, strengthens and establishes us inasmuch as He has called us to be with Him in His eternal glory.

Holy Bible says God created man with dust of the ground and because man transgressed God's command man returns dead to the earth. The sufferings in this world are part of man's life and they cannot be avoided no matter how much one tries to get rid of them. Man's body is redeemed only after it is dead like the seed that is sown in the ground dies first and then rises to new life.

What if an organization, which loathes to be called as "religion", because it has no system of faith and worship, and does not owe allegiance to any God or supernatural being teaches that man's suffering can be alleviated with the enlightenment he receives after many years of meditation under a tree or on a mountain? I would prefer calling it as an "organization", who formulated some tenets that appear to be right in their view. They are rather more inclined to dwell on political structure, and philosophical teachings rather than religion or Godly ways.

There was a man who lived in affluent family in his prime youth, and he thought by his asceticism he would gain enlightenment sufficient to live rest of his life happily. The prince left his family and friends and went and spent much time to find ways, not only to get himself rid of sufferings in this life, but teach ways to others to get themselves rid of their sufferings. He found none of such happiness that he desired, and then went and sat under a tree for many years and rose to spend rest of his forty years teaching that there are sufferings in this world, and one can overcome sufferings by adopting four noble truths.

The founder was an Indian prince, who lived an affluent life for 29 years, saw on one of his journeys an old man, a sick man, a poor man and a dead body. Their sufferings on the earth touched his passions immensely and, therefore, he left his wife and children to seek enlightenment through self-denial, which is asceticism. He tried but failed miserably, and then he made another attempt of sitting under a tree vowing not to move until he received enlightenment. Surprisingly, after many days he rose as enlightened one. He had 45 years more to get enlightened and to get rid of the sufferings, and he spent all that time in achieving that goal while he also established a community of monks.

It was about 2500 years ago that this organization came into existence and it had transformations from giving up of their initial thoughts of observance of rituals, and worship of deities in favor of meditations. The said organization teaches that sufferings can be overcome by adopting four noble truths that found their ways into their sacred texts based on the thought process of men. What does that organization teach?

Their teachings do not emphasize on believing in God, but they are more of concern for human nature and one's final realization about oneself. The founder taught that it is important to understand the true nature of the world and be practical rather than sticking onto the teachings superficially. Speculations about the existence of God the afterlife and about the nature of the universe are anathemas to them.

The organization insists on concentrating on what their founder understood as the four noble truths. Those four truths perhaps pave the way for alleviation from suffering. Those four noble truths, according to him are…

1. Life is full of sufferings
2. Desire and attachment cause suffering
3. Man can stop suffering
4. And suffering can be stopped by adopting eight fold path

What a vanity of realization is that after being enlightened he comes to conclusion that life is full of sufferings, and sufferings are caused by desire and attachment, and the resolution is that man can stop suffering and that by man-made eight-fold paths.

Who has known the mind of God, and who has the strength to stop thunders, storms, hurricanes and volcanoes? Who has set the boundaries of seas that they could come only up to the point that they have been authorized to come! Ah! If only man could alleviate the pain, sufferings there would have been no medical facilities, and deaths by serious diseases. A false consolation does not solve the problem, but reliance on the Truth of the Knowledge of the Holy Scriptures affords consolation.

Their eight-fold-path is:

1. A True and right knowledge that complies with their beliefs
2. A True and right intention
3. A True and correct speech
4. A True and correct action
5. A True and appropriate livelihood
6. A True and correct endeavors
7. A True and correct mindfulness
8. A True and correct concentration

The belief that one can overcome sufferings by meditation or sitting under a tree is quite contrary to the teachings of the Holy Bible. It is dark world where it is for us to shed light with knowledge of the truth and that truth is found in the Holy Scriptures. It is to understand that life is mixture of happiness and sufferings.

Just while typing this message I received a message that one of my aunts died of terminally ill disease. However, my faith gives me hope that I will be with the Lord immediately I die; and one day I can see her in eternity. This is Christian hope and there are many verses in the Bible that give us hope of happiness in life after death.

Seeking enlightenment on the sufferings and how they can be alleviated does not produce any profitable solution except that the one who endeavors to find ways to alleviate pain and suffering spends quite a great deal of time and energy in vain to find solutions to such problems. No matter how one meditates; being with family or by deserting family, one surely would spend time in vain in such pursuits.

Bible teaches that along with suffering comes much joy in the Lord even while we are in this world dominated by satanic activities. There was a man named Job, who suffered greatly in his life but finally he was blessed. There is none who suffers pain or agony or persecution, who would not be blessed ultimately. Trying to escape from sufferings is not the way of life, but facing the realities and seeking to overcome them or endure them with the help of God is the way of life.

Psalmist writes

"Surely he shall deliver thee from the snare of the fowler, and from the noisome pestilence" (Psalms 91:3)

There shall no evil befall thee, neither shall any plague come nigh thy dwelling. For he shall give his angels charge over thee, to keep thee in all thy ways. They shall bear thee up in their hands, lest thou dash thy foot against a stone. (Psalms 91:10-12)

When a believer in Christ is in need of help God is right there to help him. When he accidentally falls from a cliff God sends His angels to hold him up lest he should dash his foot against a stone. That does not mean one should jump from cliff to prove God's word or challenge Him. Proving God is like insulting Jesus when He was on the cross. People challenged Lord Jesus Christ to come down from the cross if He was God. Not that Jesus could not come down from the cross if wished so but the purpose of His coming to this world would have been defeated then.

No matter what the sufferings are; there is comfort in God. The universe is created for all alike; irrespective of one is believer or unbeliever. The Law of Gravity, for example, would not have compassion on a believer, who jumps off cliff in challenging tone. What is achieved in believing in God is that man is delivered from hitting the rock on the ground if he accidentally fell from the cliff. A believer does not get neglected by God when he prays to be rescued.

Suffering cannot be avoided but the redemption from suffering is afforded by God for those who believe in Him; and it is possible through simple belief in Lord Jesus Christ. It is not by siting under a tree for many years, or climbing thousands of steps on a hill to reach a god.

God is omniscient. King Solomon, the wisest man ever lived on the earth, realized this fact and said who can build a temple, large enough for God to live in, because the heaven is His throne and the earth is His footstool.

Self-denial or self-inflicting or to attain enlightenment sitting under a tree are not the resolutions to overcome sufferings, but it is the realization that dependence on God that will help us get rid of situations which result in sorrow and suffering. If God allows suffering the joy would be in accepting what He allows in our lives, rather than making attempts in human capacity to resist the natural laws set by Him in their places.

There is nothing that a man can achieve by getting enlightened how to get rid of suffering but it is wise to spend time to find resolutions for the sufferings which are already in the world.

Man may spend whole life to attain this knowledge and yet he dies in not more than realization that there is suffering, and it is futile to get such enlightenment about the sufferings or to find ways to alleviate them.

Neither enough money, nor any pleasure can bring happiness in man's life, until he first realizes that all is vanity, and everything is transient and temporal. The leader and founder of this organization, who had enlightenment to find remedies to overcome sufferings was said to have died in his old age of 80 years suffering dysentery, sharp and deadly pains.

It does not mean that man should not strive to earn money or happiness, or be joyful in his life. There is no negativity in realizing the fact that man is born in this world crying and he is sent away from this world with cry from close family members and friends.

What bothers me is that a man who is born in affluent family deserts his family and friends and goes and spends much time to find ways to get rid of sufferings in this life, but finds none, and then later goes and sits under a tree for many years and rises to spend forty more years of his life teaching that there are sufferings in this world, and ultimately dies of dysentery, sharp and deadly pains. Of course, there are variant reports of the causes of his death devoid of reliable documents and sources.

I am so comfortable in knowing that Lord Jesus Christ died on the cross; He was buried and His body did not see corruption and He rose from the grave on the third day. I surely boast of myself that I belong to Him, who defeated death, pain and suffering. He called me a child of God, and I am given the privilege of calling Him as Abba, Father. He has assured me that I will be in New Jerusalem, where there is no pain, no suffering and no death. Then, there is no reason why I should seek my destiny at any other place or in any other religion than my relationship with my God. My relationship excels every other religion and the way Lord Jesus Christ has provided for me is the only True way. He is the Way, the Truth and the Life.

It is interesting to read a passage about truth as they understand:

"There is truth in the stone, for the stone is here; and no power in the world, no god, no man, no demon, can destroy its existence. But the stone has no consciousness. There is truth in the plant and its life can expand; the plant grows and blossoms and bears fruit. Its beauty is marvelous, but it has no consciousness. There is truth in the animal; it moves about and perceives its surroundings; it distinguishes and learns to choose. There is consciousness, but it is not yet the consciousness of Truth. It is a consciousness of self only".

Let us read Holy Scriptures from the Bible and see if any one stop the wrath of God, and can He destroy the mountains, if He is despised? Of the many passages in the Bible one that I picked to quote here is from Deuteronomy 32:16-22. The truth is here…

"They stirred him to jealousy with strange gods; with abominations they provoked him to anger. They sacrificed to demons that were no gods, to gods they had never known, to new gods that had come recently, whom your fathers had never dreaded. You were unmindful of the Rock that bore you, and you forgot the God who gave you birth. "The LORD saw it and spurned them, because of the provocation of his sons and his daughters. And he said, 'I will hide my face from them; I will see what their end will be, for they are a perverse generation, children in whom is no faithfulness. They have made me jealous with what is no god; they have provoked me to anger with their idols. So I will make them jealous with those who are no people; I will provoke them to anger with a foolish nation. For a fire is kindled by my anger, and it burns to the depths of Sheol, devours the earth and its increase, and sets on fire the foundations of the mountains" (Deuteronomy 32:16-22 ESV)

To utter surprise their teaching is that man can work out salvation for him and for others as well. Their teachings are known as "Dharma", which is the underlying truth. "Karma" involves in inescapable results of our actions. "Re-birth" in affluent families or spend future in poverty depending on "Karma" that one resorts to and that there is no god, who interferes with "Karma" of any person. Their concepts and beliefs are far beyond my acceptance. I believe Lord Jesus Christ shows me the Way. He is the Truth, the Way and the Life.

The presence of soul in a man is illusion according to their teaching, and yet they say that there is re-birth. The living being is considered as a composition of various parts similar to the parts assembled in a computer, which would deteriorate as the time lapses, and a new computer is bought in its place. It seems old computer's soul is not found but a new computer comes into existence. It is contrary to their teaching that re-birth, according to them, occurs without soul. If it is new, it is new and not a re-birth and if it is re-birth, then there should have been a soul which would have re-birth; if at all that conception is right.

Another comparison is that when a candle is in the final stages of extinguishing man takes a new candle and lights it up with the help of the old candle and thereby there is probably a continuity of light. These comparisons are so flimsy and unreliable. A new candle does not need the help of an old candle. It could be lit up with a new matchstick, and when that is done the old candle gets extinguished fully. This comparison or the thinking that old gets extinguished fully is trivial and beyond my comprehension. I wish I had time to refute every such trivial comparison!

Holy Bible is not a book of fiction but of Spiritual knowledge containing inspired scriptures. The deaths of various saints recorded in the Bible shows us how true the life and afterlife are! King David, who was called as a man after the heart of God died almost like an 'invalid', while Jacob's death was so pleasant.

"And when the time drew near that Israel must die, he called his son Joseph and said to him, 'If now I have found favor in your sight, put your hand under my thigh and promise to deal kindly and truly with me. Do not bury me in Egypt, but let me lie with my fathers. Carry me out of Egypt and bury me in their burying place.' He answered, 'I will do as you have said.' And he said, 'Swear to me'; and he swore to him. Then Israel bowed himself upon the head of his bed" (Genesis 47:29-31 ESV)

"When Jacob finished commanding his sons, he drew up his feet into the bed and breathed his last and was gathered to his people" (Genesis 49:33 ESV)

I am content to believe in the infallible Holy Scriptures which say:

"For if the dead are not raised, not even Christ has been raised. And if Christ has not been raised, your faith is futile and you are still in your sins. Then those also who have fallen asleep in Christ have perished" (1 Corinthians 15:16-18 ESV)

THE RESURRECTED BODY

"But someone will ask, "How are the dead raised? With what kind of body do they come?" You foolish person! What you sow does not come to life unless it dies. And what you sow is not the body that is to be, but a bare kernel, perhaps of wheat or of some other grain. But God gives it a body as he has chosen, and to each kind of seed its own body" (1 Corinthians 15:35-38 ESV)

Lord Jesus died a humiliating death upon the cross bearing our sin upon Himself, even though He was sinless, and without any blemish. It was for our salvation that we may not die eternally. There is no re-birth; but a new life to live eternally with Lord Jesus Christ in a body that is not made of hands but a building from God, eternal in heavens. There is more a re-birth in poverty or destroyable dusty body.

"For we know that if the tent that is our earthly home is destroyed, we have a building from God, a house not made with hands, eternal in the heavens" 2 Corinthians 5:1

Disclaimer: This presentation is my personal view about my beliefs, and not a condemnation of any other beliefs/faiths of any other religions. No offence is meant to any individual, or religion, or any organization practicing any other beliefs than mine.

Except for study and personal use, copying the contents of this article either in full or in part for any other purpose is strictly prohibited.

CHAPTER 3

MY TESTIMONY

Dear Brother/Sister:

When it comes to writing about one's own testimony, one wonders where one should start and where to end. That is exactly is the predicament I face inasmuch as I have so much to write about myself.

Hailing from India and born in a Christian middle class family, I was raised in a Christian background and had my education in Christian Institutions, where I had the privilege to learn much about Christianity and Jesus Christ. I accepted Jesus Christ as my personal savior and acknowledged HIM as my Lord, when I was a boy of 13 years and since then I saw a change in my life.

This then is the message, which I have heard of HIM, of the Son of God, Jesus Christ, whom I declare unto you, that God is light, and in him is no darkness at all. Jesus Christ was sent from above to save sinners like me, died for my sake bearing my sins upon himself on the cross of Calvary in order to redeem me from the bondage of sin, and if I confess I will not perish but have eternal life.

It is this Lord Jesus, our "Good shepherd», who manifests to us the name and nature of our Great living God. It is right, then, that to this dark world the great God should be represented as pure and perfect light. I obeyed the Word of God and accepted Jesus as my LORD.

Colossians 1:15-18 He is the image of the invisible God, the firstborn over all creation. For by Him all things were created that are in heaven and that are on earth, visible and invisible, whether thrones or dominions or principalities or powers. All things were created through Him and for Him. And He is before all things, and in Him all things consist. And He is the head of the body, the church, who is the beginning, the firstborn from the dead, that in all things He may have the preeminence.

When I was young, I had no option but to leave home and work at a very distant place from my home town for several years. This helped me to associate with several categories of people from several parts of India. Somehow, from the time I was employed I fell sick several times. Again, this helped me to share the Word of God with co-patients in hospitals. God helped me to tell people who Jesus Christ is. I gladly and boldly declared about the love of Jesus Christ, wherever I was.

I cannot forget the situation I was in when I fell totally unconscious on my chair because I was seriously ill, and the way God helped me by finding people to carry me with the chair from the living room to the ambulance and then to the hospital for treatment. This reminds me the promise God gave me through a believer who cited:

Isaiah 46:4 And even to your old age I am he; and even to hoar hairs will I carry you: I have made, and I will bear; even I will carry, and will deliver you.

It is indeed true that God carried me all through these years until this day. I praise him and worship Him. More than that I boast in saying that I have a living God, who I can depend upon and who sent His one only one Son, Jesus Christ, who died for me on the cross of Calvary, was buried and rose from the dead on the third day, and later ascended in to heaven.

Now, when I drive my car early in the morning on the over bridge of Interstate highway, I usually turn my head to right to catch a glimpse of the beaming rays emitting out from the head lights of fast moving cars in different lanes.

My heart rejoices, my spirit soars so high and my soul praises my God for giving me such privilege to watch that scene. It was because I worked at a place where I thronged to catch glimpse of a light ray from an electric bulb, which was not available anywhere near at least within a radius of eight to ten kilometers.

But now when I look towards the sky in the night to watch the twinkling lights beaming out from the stars, and meditate on the ONE who created them, I would not say that there is no God. How blessed I am that that can view these STARS and wonderful galaxy from any part of the world, not just from the over bridge of an Interstate Highway.

Bible deals severely with those who say there is no God.

Psalms 14:1 The fool has said in his heart, There is no God. They are corrupt, they have done abominable works, there is none that does good.

The same is repeated in:

Psalm 53:1 Wicked, and an ungodly persons will say that there is no God! Pity on them!! Where would they go if God does not help them?

They would rather be groping in darkness.

I am saved by the grace of our Lord Jesus Christ. If I am living today, having recovered from several sicknesses, it is only because of His mercy and nothing but His mercy. I owe my Lord, service and worship all the rest of my days. Let me assert that Jesus Christ is the Son of God. Our God is Almighty. He is the Alpha and He is the Omega. There was none like HIM before, nor there will any be after. I worship HIM. I glorify HIS name. Praise is to our God, in the name of His Son Jesus Christ.

Incredible as it appears, years rolled by and I realize I have not done much for my Lord Jesus Christ. I was completely immersed in family life and I acknowledge that I did not give much importance for working for the spreading of the Word of God.

Before His ascension into heaven, Lord Jesus Christ commanded His disciples,

Matthew 28:19-20 ...go and make disciples of all nations, baptizing them in the name of the Father and of the Son and of the Holy Spirit, and teaching them to obey everything I have commanded you. And Surely I am with you always, to the very end of the age.

The following verse, which Jesus said in John 15:4, was like a warning to me that I should not lose any more time and bear fruit for HIM.

John 15:4 Remain in me, and I will remain in you. No branch can bear fruit by itself; it must remain in the vine. Neither can you bear fruit unless you remain in me.

Now that I have great longing for working for our Lord Jesus Christ I started making these pages so that people may read and believe that Lord Jesus Christ is the WAY, the TRUTH, and the LIFE.

This then is what Jesus said...

John 6:37 All that the Father gives me will come to me, and whoever comes to me I will never drive away.

John 14:11 Believe me when I say that I am in the Father and the Father is in me; or at least believe on the evidence of the miracles themselves.»

John 15:16 You did not choose me, but I chose you and appointed you to go and bear fruit—fruit that will last. Then the Father will give you whatever you ask in my name.»

John 3:3 I tell you the truth, no one can see the kingdom of God unless he is born again.

John 3:16 For God so loved the world that he gave his one and only Son, that whoever believes in him shall not perish but have eternal life.

Romans 6:23 For the wages of sin is death, but the gift of God is eternal life in Christ Jesus our Lord.

Romans 8:1 Therefore, there is no condemnation for those who are in Christ Jesus.

If you confess your sins to Lord Jesus Christ and accept Him as your personal Savior, you will be saved. Please do not delay. Today is the right time to allow Lord Jesus to come into your heart.

MY TESTIMONY PART II

Born into this world to Christian parents of middle class, and having been raised with Christian values, I have tasted the love of my Lord and Savior Jesus Christ until now, and have great hope that I will taste His love forever.

To the requirement that Bible demands from everyone that unless a man is born of water and Spirit he cannot see the kingdom of God, I have been from above when I was of 13 years of age, and after few years had immersion baptism.

"Jesus answered and said unto him, Verily, verily, I say unto thee, Except a man be born again, he cannot see the kingdom of God. Nicodemus saith unto him, How can a man be born when he is old? Can he enter the second time into his mother's womb, and be born? Jesus answered, Verily, verily, I say unto thee, Except a man be born of water and of the Spirit, he cannot enter into the kingdom of God" (John 3:3-5 KJV)

Dust that I am formed of and dust that I will return to, and yet I have great assurance from God that I will be with Him forever and ever in my glorified body from the day the Lord returns. As John writes, "Amen. Even so, come, Lord Jesus", I do say that same in response to the Lord's assurance recorded in Revelation 22:20...

"Surely I come quickly. Amen. Even so, come, Lord Jesus" (Revelation 22:20 KJV)

Circumstances necessitated that I should leave home when I was 19 years old to join Indian Air Force. Being weak in health I always suffered from some kind ailment. Unable to cope with the requirements of Indian Air Force, I was granted discharge at my request from IAF on compassionate grounds.

After joining my parents in Hyderabad in Andhra Pradesh, India, I worked for State Government for two years and from there I joined Indian Railways and have had successful life for many years. In the meanwhile my kidneys failed and I had Kidney transplant in India in 1997. By the grace of God everything went on well, and as on this day, it is 22 years since I had kidney transplant. It is, indeed a miracle, and I am living by the grace of God.

Having received opportunity to lead a better life in the most wonderful country, I had taken voluntary retirement from Indian Railways, and migrated with family to USA in 2000. Now, I am not only a citizen of heaven, but also of USA that I love wholeheartedly.

By the grace of God we are all doing well and serving the LORD to the best of our capacity.

☐

CHAPTER 4

SEARCH THE SCRIPTURES

These were nobler than those in Thessalonica, in that they received the word with all readiness of mind, and searched the scriptures daily, whether those things were so. (Acts 17:11)

The Bible lays importance in proving Scriptures with Scriptures abd by searching the Bible thoroughly, instead of accepting diverse interpretations of Biblical truths straightway. The fact is that not all Christians know how to interpret the Scriptures in right way and in addition Bible says there are many false prophets and false preachers, who divert believers into confusion.

Many even do not accept that Jesus is the Son of God, and the Word became flesh. Bible lays importance in rightly divide the Scriptures. Study to show yourself approved unto God, a workman, who does not need not to be ashamed, rightly dividing the word of truth. (cf. 2 Timothy 2:15)

" 1Beloved, do not believe every spirit, but test the spirits to see whether they are from God, for many false prophets have gone out into the world. 2By this you know the Spirit of God: every spirit that confesses that Jesus Christ has come in the flesh is from God, 3and every spirit that does not confess Jesus is not from God. This is the spirit of the antichrist, which you heard was coming and now is in the world already" (1 John 4:1-3 ESV)

"…test everything; hold fast what is good" (1 Thessalonians 5:21 ESV)

Apostle Paul traveled from Philippi to Amphipolis and then to Apollonia and to Thessalonica, during one of his three missionary journeys, a total about one hundred miles in several days, in all probability by foot or cart, and went to synagogue of Jews, according to his custom, as we read in Acts 17:1. He reasoned with Jews for three weeks, about the necessity of Jesus to die for mankind, from the writings of Isaiah chapter 53, and Psalm 22 etc. He reasoned that unless Jesus who was the Son of God, die a substitutionary death on behalf of mankind, reconciliation between the Father and the mankind was not possible.

It was that Jesus, who was the Messiah, the savior of the world that Paul was speaking about. The result of His preaching was quite good in that certain of them believed and followed Paul and his associate Silas. In addition a great multitude, and women who worshipped Greek gods consorted with Paul and Silas. However, there were also Jews, who did not believe in their preaching, were moved with envy. They gathered unto them "lewd fellows of the baser sort" (cf. Acts 17:5), and along with them set the entire city on an uproar, and assaulted the house of Jason.

These rebellious Jews spread the news that Paul and Silas were doing things that are contrary to the decrees of Caesar. They with their malicious intentions said that Paul and Silas were speaking about another king – Jesus. The confused the multitudes with falsification of the realities. Realizing danger for Paul and Silas, brethren at Thessalonica sent Paul and Silas to Berea.

As soon as Paul and Silas reached Berea they went into synagogue of the Jews, who were nobler than those in

Thessalonica. They received the Word of God with all readiness of mind and daily examined them to see if they were really so as Paul and Silas preached. It was the right way of believing in the Word of God; not just listen, and believe straightway, but to examine in the light of the Scriptures.

Many preachers/teachers interpret Scriptures erroneously, and therefore, it is of utmost importance that after hearing the word of God, one should search the Scriptures and compare with the relative prophecies in the Old Testament to see if they were really so as preached.

There was much fruit produced by the preaching of Paul and Silas at Berea. Many men and women believed in the Word of God, and in Lord Jesus Christ.

However, the trouble started again as Jews from Thessalonica went to Berea and there they caused commotion among people. Brethren there sent Paul as far as to the sea, but Silas and Timothy remained there. Later on as Paul desired Silas and Timothy joined Paul and Athens.

☐

CHAPTER 5

THE LORD'S SUPPER

Legalism has divided the Body of Christ/the Church into several parts/groups within the Christendom interpreting many Bible verses differently. One such issue is with the interpretation of the Scriptures about the Lord's Supper. There is much dispute among several Christians as to how the Lord's Supper is to be celebrated. Some of the pestering questions are as follows:

Should the bread be an unleavened bread or just an ordinary bread?

Should the bread be one loaf or several wafers?

Should a single cup be used or multiple cups?

What should be the contents of the 'the cup'?

Is the Lord's Supper a worship, or remembrance of the Lord's death?, etc.

Matthew Chapter 26:1-75 is a lengthy chapter; however, it greatly helps to read the whole chapter. Key verses are Matthew 26:26-29.

The Lord's Supper is a fellowship meal in memory of Lord Jesus Christ's sacrifice of Himself on the cross of Calvary on behalf of mankind. It is not a mourning time, but is a time to remember the Lord Jesus Christ's substitutionary death on the cross of Calvary for the sake of mankind. It is to assert visibly that Jesus died on the cross for our sins, and that whosoever believes in His death and resurrection will be saved from eternal damnation.

The bread that was used in the Passover meal was necessarily an unleavened bread in compliance to the Old Testament Scriptures.

"And they shall eat the flesh in that night, roast with fire, and unleavened bread; and with bitter herbs they shall eat it" (Exodus 12:8)

However, the Lord's Supper was instituted after the Passover meal. Although the bread that was used in Passover meal on that night was unleavened bread, the bread that was used while instituting Lord's Supper does not seem to be unleavened bread. When such disputes come up it necessitates us to refer to Greek word from which English word is translated.

"Now the first day of the feast of unleavened bread the disciples came to Jesus, saying unto him, Where wilt thou that we prepare for thee to eat the passover?" (Matthew 26:17)

"And as they were eating, Jesus took bread, and blessed it, and brake it, and gave it to the disciples, and said, Take, eat; this is my body" (Matthew 26:26)

In Matthew26:17, when Jesus used the unleavened bread during Passover meal, the Greek word used is Greek Strong's# 106 "azumos", which refers to unleavened bread, while the Greek word used for Lord's Supper in verse 26:26 is Greek Strong's# 706 "artos", which simply means common loaf.

Leaven in the Bible commonly symbolizes sin, and rightly so, the Old Testament saints used unleavened bread to celebrate Passover meal. However, New Testament believers are not bound to use unleavened bread in the

Lord's Supper. Therefore, it is too legalism to insist on using unleavened bread in the Lord's Supper.

The Lord's Supper was instituted by Lord Jesus Christ after celebration of Passover festival.

26 Now as they were eating, Jesus took bread, and after blessing it broke it and gave it to the disciples, and said, "Take, eat; this is my body."27And he took a cup, and when he had given thanks he gave it to them, saying, "Drink of it, all of you, 28for this is my blood of the covenant, which is poured out for many for the forgiveness of sins.29I tell you I will not drink again of this fruit of the vine until that day when I drink it new with you in my Father's kingdom." (Matthew 26:26-29 ESV)

The first phrase in this key passage is "Now as they were eating". It is evident from this phrase that the Lord's Supper was instituted as they were eating Passover meal. It is at that time that Lord Jesus took bread and blessed it.

Lord Jesus then broke it and gave it to His disciples and said "Take, eat; this is my body". Was that real body of Jesus? No, it was symbolic. In order to remember His body that was broken for the salvation of mankind, He commanded to break the bread and distribute among themselves.

Likewise, He took the cup and when he had given thanks He gave to them, "drink of it, all of you". When the Lord instituted the Lord's Supper, the cup was distributed among His twelve disciples, making it a visible example as to how His followers in the later days, months and years to distribute among themselves.

A small cup was enough to share from by His twelve disciples, but if by legalism, a small cup was to be used for distribution of the cup among a large number of believers, say one thousand in a gathering, it obviously is not enough, but surely demands a larger vessel or necessitates to divide the contents of the cup or vessel into smaller cups for distribution.

It is beyond doubt that Lord Jesus was telling to drink of the cup and not the cup itself. Cup is solid in state, and therefore, even the verb "drink" cannot be used, if the cup was to be drunken, but it should have been to eat the cup, which is absurd in meaning.

Therefore, it is quite clear that Lord Jesus was telling His disciples drink the contents of the cup and the contents have to be distributed among His disciples.

CHAPTER 6

THE WORD OF GOD

"For this cause also thank we God without ceasing, because, when ye received the word of God which ye heard of us, ye received it not as the word of men, but as it is in truth, the word of God, which effectually worketh also in you that believe" (1 Thessalonians 2:13)

The Word of God is the Word that the Almighty God spoke through forty writers lived in different periods of time, spanning nearly 1500 years, and yet they all dwelt on one central theme that God is love. God of heavens, who is known by several names, especially as "I AM THAT I AM", out breathed the inspired scriptures, which are immutable and inerrant.

People of different languages have translated the Word of God into their languages, and while doing so, some words, may have inadvertently crept into cause misunderstanding of certain words, and their interpretation, and yet the central theme and the intention of God has not changed.

It is not the word of man, but it is the Word of God. Apostle Paul addressing Thessalonians says that when they heard the Word of God from them they believed the Word of God. They did not receive it as the word of men, but as the word of God. The Word of God is the Truth, and it words effectually in all those who believe in the word of God.

Even those Atheist Jews, who said the Word of God contains fables or myths changed their opinion when they are required to say their share in the land of Israel, and their lineage. Their share is recorded in Ezekiel 48:1-35

He who believes in the word of God is like a tree planted by the waters. That tree never gets dried because it is continually fed with water. It is always lively and greenish. A believer who has fellowship with God and believes the Word of God is like unto the tree that is planted on the banks of rivers.

☐

CHAPTER 7

THE WORD OF TRUTH

In whom ye also trusted, after that ye heard the word of truth, the gospel of your salvation: in whom also after that ye believed, ye were sealed with that Holy Spirit of promise, (Ephesians 1:13)

There are four elements involved in this verse…

- In whom you also trusted
- After that ye heard the word of truth
- In whom also after that ye believed
- You were sealed with that Holy Spirit of promise

What a great assurance for believers in Christ!

The last phrase attracts our attention greater than anyone, that we were sealed with the Holy Spirit of Promise. Our salvation is never lost. We heard the Gospel of Jesus Christ first. It is the Word of Truth.

After hearing the word of truth we believed, and then we are sealed with the Holy Spirit of Promise to be with the Lord forever and ever in eternity.

Our resurrection to be with the Lord is sure; more so, with the redemption of our bodies in incorruptible state and in glorious form in the twinkling of an eye, when the Lord comes again.

Unlike, those unbelievers who resurrect to be judged and condemned our state is never to be condemned but to be conformed to the image of Christ. The contrast is between the Jewish believers and the Gentiles believers. In Christ neither Jew nor Gentile is separate, but all are one. The believers are altogether called "the one new man". This was mystery in the Old Testament period, but revealed in the New Testament. The first point "in whom you trusted" points to the Gentile believers, who are given the same privilege as of Jews

☐

CHAPTER 8

APPROVED UNTO GOD

"Study to show yourself approved unto God, a workman that need not to be ashamed, rightly dividing the word of truth" (2 Timothy 2:15)

Apostle Paul says…

"According to the grace of God given to me, like a skilled master builder I laid a foundation, and someone else is building upon it. Let each one take care how he builds upon it. 11For no one can lay a foundation other than that which is laid, which is Jesus Christ. Now if anyone builds on the foundation with gold, silver, precious stones, wood, hay, straw— each one's work will become manifest, for the Day will disclose it, because it will be revealed by fire, and the fire will test what sort of work each one has done. If the work that anyone has built on the foundation survives, he will receive a reward. If anyone's work is burned up, he will suffer loss, though he himself will be saved, but only as through fire" (1 Corinthians 3:10-15 ESV)

Paul also says…

"Set your minds on things that are above, not on things that are on earth" (Colossians 3:2 ESV)

Now, he instructs Timothy, a fellow preacher, whom Paul treated as his son,

"Do your best to present yourself to God as one approved, a worker who has no need to be ashamed, rightly handling the word of truth" (2 Timothy 2:15 ESV)

Ponder on few phrases here… "Do your best"(ESV) — ("Study to shew" [KJV]), — "present yourself to God as one approved" (ESV) — ("approved unto God"[KJV])

It is all the same. Do your best to present yourself approved unto God as one, who is not ashamed to do the work of God and rightly handling the Word of Truth. The admonition is to see that we set our minds on the spiritual things that are in heaven, rather than material things that are in earth.

Paul testifies that by the grace that was given to him, like a skilled master builder he laid a foundation, which is quite apart from "Judaism". He hoped someone else would be building upon it.

He says everyone has the responsibility to build upon the foundation he laid. It is the Lord Jesus Christ, who helps build upon the rock, and that rock is the Lord Himself.

Lord Jesus Christ is the head of the Church, and all the believers collectively are the members of His body. No one can lay a foundation that which is laid by the Lord Jesus Christ Himself, using people like His disciples, and Apostle Paul.

Everyone else's efforts to build upon one's own wisdom, or with gold, or silver, or with precious stones, or wood, or hay, or straw, will become known, and publicly denounced. They will all be put to shame. There comes a day when all false teachers will be revealed, and their works will be revealed by fire.

The fire wil test the kind of work each one has done. Everyone who builds upon the foundation that is laid by Lord Jesus Christ, through His apostles, will survive and they will be rewarded by the Lord. The loss that one suffers because of his work is burned up, will be immense and colossal, although he might be saved, by the test administered by the Lord, only through fire.

The main emphasis is to turn others over to the Lord from the influences of worldly desires, and away from unprofitable things of the world. In standing for the Lord, and proclaiming God's word, a believer has to make sure that he fulfills the provisions of Romans 13:1-2 which says…

"1Let every person be subject to the governing authorities. For there is no authority except from God, and those that exist have been instituted by God. 2Therefore whoever resists the authorities resists what God has appointed, and those who resist will incur judgment" (ESV)

Make sure that believer does not violate Government laws, and prevailing provisions under the law of the land. The encouragement given in 2 Timothy 2:15 does not undermine the provisions of Romans 13:1-2.

It does not give blanket license to disobey the laws of the land, unless Government follows anti-Godly policies, and terrorizes its own citizens, quite contrary to the provisions laid down in the bible

☐

CHAPTER 9

TO BE PERFECT

"That the man of God may be perfect, thoroughly furnished unto all good works" (2 Timothy 3:17 KJV)

"That the man of God may be complete, equipped for every good work" (2 Timothy 3:17 ESV). The phrase "may be perfect" or "may be complete" poses great challenge! It is, indeed very hard for a man with divine thoughts countered constantly in his mind to become perfect in every respect.

It is, indeed, very hard to cope with the conflicting thoughts warring with one another to settle down to the divine counsel unless man takes refuge in the sacred Scriptures.

Even Godly man needs God's help every moment in his life to lead an extremely good life pleasing to the Lord. It is, therefore, Paul writes in Ephesians 6:10-18 to be life Christian Soldiers –armored with spiritual shields against fiery darts of temptations being hurled constantly by Satan.

Even after believing in Christ, man needs God's help every day to live and overcome the temptations of this world. The devil did not leave even Lord Jesus from tempting Him; however, the Lord being the Son of God, impeccable, overcome temptations quoting Scriptures to the devil.

2 Timothy 3:17 continuation of verse 16. There is a chance of misinterpreting verse 17 if it is not read as a continuation of verse 16.

Together, the passage reads as follows:

"All Scripture is breathed out by God and profitable for teaching, for reproof, for correction, and for training in righteousness, that the man of God may be complete, equipped for every good work. 2 Timothy 3:15-17

For a man to be complete and be equipped for every good work, he needs to depend on the whole Bible, which contains sacred Scriptures, which were inspired and out breathed by Almighty God, and they are given to man to profit from them and teach, to reproof, to correct, and for training in righteousness.

If a man do his best to the teachings of the Bible and obedient to God, then he will surely come very close to being perfect.

As the Scriptures say perfect sanctification comes only when the body of man is redeemed from the grave and changes into glorious body at the twinkling of an eye, when Lord Jesus Comes again. Until then, man needs to depend upon God and the sacred Scriptures available to us in the form the Bible. (cf. 1 Corinthians 15:42-56; 1 Thessalonians 4:16-18; 1 Thessalonians 5:23)

CHAPTER 10

FOR DOCTRINE

"All scripture is given by inspiration of God, and is profitable for doctrine, for reproof, for correction, for instruction in righteousness" (2 Timothy 3:16)

Before making what seems to be a conclusive remark here in 2 Timothy 3:16, Apostle Paul speaks of the "last days" and how bad those days will be in the verses before this verse.

From the very first verse he speaks of imminent perilous times. The Sacred inspired Scriptures that Paul wrote at the behest of our Lord Jesus, whom He always adored and worked for, say that there will be hypocrites, formal professors, and false preachers in the "last days".

Bible says, "All scripture is given by the inspiration of God…" Every verse in the Bible is Scripture out breathed by the LORD God, Jehovah and every scriptures in the Bible is "profitable for doctrine, for reproof, for correction, for instruction in righteousness".

Yet, there are many Christians, who believe in New Testament alone, and ignore the truth that is in the Old Testament. Much of the Truth evades those that ignore Old Testament.

Old Testament is like the basis and foundational truth of the Almighty God and His power, His creation, and His choosing of one Nation, which, He called as His Nation and the people therein as His people. Apostle Paul likened Mosaic Law to that of a School Master. God spoke to different people in different periods of time in different ways. His ways are marvelous, and His thoughts are higher than ours.

Bible contains factual occurrences, and none is a fable, or a myth. They are historical events, and contains prophecies. 2 Timothy 3:1-17 dwells much on the 'last days'.

One thing to be noted is that every age appears to be the 'last days' and yet the end is not there yet. The Holy Scriptures are ever fresh, dealing with man's past, present and the future and never could a man despise the thought that he is living in the 'last days'.

Paul mentions, interestingly, two names in 2 Timothy 3:8, and they are "Jannes and Jambres", who opposed Moses. These names are not found anywhere in the Bible other than in 2 Timothy 3:18.

However, they are believed to be two of the magicians Pharaoh called for in order to oppose Moses and Aaron, who went into the court of Pharaoh demanding the release of the children of Israel from the bondage of slavery. Jews believed they were sons of Balaam.

1 Maccabees 9:36 makes a reference to these names. Historian Josephus makes a mention about them while mentioning the names of sons of Amaraeus.

As a precursor to the demand, they obeyed the LORD to show their dependence on God, on whose command they were there to challenge Pharaoh. Aaron dropped the rod of Moses on the ground, as the LORD commanded by the mouth of Moses, and it became a serpent.

Soon, Pharaoh also tried to show his power by calling the wise men, sorcerers and the magicians of Egypt. They also did similar act by their secret arts; everyone dropped his rod, and each became a serpent, but Aaron's rod swallowed magicians' rods.

The two names (Janes and Jambres) mentioned in 2 Timothy 3:8 were the two magicians, who dropped their rods on the ground and they became serpents. However, Aaron rod swallowed every rod of every magician, thus showing superiority of living God through Moses and Aaron.

"So Moses and Aaron went to Pharaoh and did just as the Lord commanded. Aaron cast down his staff before Pharaoh and his servants, and it became a serpent.

Then Pharaoh summoned the wise men and the sorcerers, and they, the magicians of Egypt, also did the same by their secret arts. For each man cast down his staff, and they became serpents. But Aaron's staff swallowed up their staffs" (Exodus 7:10-12 ESV)

The point here is that in the last days people of such opposing nature will come up to withstand the Truth of the knowledge of the living God. While writing to Thessalonians Paul says…

"The coming of the lawless one is by the activity of Satan with all power and false signs and wonders, 10and with all wicked deception for those who are perishing, because they refused to love the truth and so be saved. 11Therefore God sends them a strong delusion, so that they may believe what is false, 12in order that all may be condemned who did not believe the truth but had pleasure in unrighteousness" (2 Thessalonians 2:9-10 ESV)

☐

CHAPTER 11

WHY JESUS WAS NOT STONED

TO DEATH?

Stoning to death of a man was violent action expressing great wrath. Stoning to death was a popular punishment executed during the Old Testament period for violating God's laws. Even not keeping Sabbath invited capital punishment during those days.

All the people had to pelt the guilty one with stones until he died. Stonings were presumably the standard form of judicial execution in biblical times Lev. 24:23; Num. 15:36; I Kings 21:13; II Chron. 24:21

It continued for many years through the ages even to the times of Jesus. However, during the period of Jesus Jews did not have power to kill anyone by stoning to death, or for that matter to execute capital punishment? Only the Roman Government had this power of executing capital punishment.

STONING is seen in the following references from the Bible

Ex. 17:4, 8:22; Num. 14:10; I Sam. 30:6; I Kings 12:18; II Chron. 10:18; Lev. 20:2, 27, 24:16; Num. 15:35; Deut. 13:11, 17:5, 21:21, 22:21; Lev. 24:16; Num. 15:35; Deut. 17:7; Lev. 24:23; Num. 15:36; I Kings 21:13; II Chron. 24:21 etc.)

Entire congregation had to pelt stones at the one declared guilty of transgression of the Law until the guilty is dead.

All the people had to pelt the guilty one with stones until he died. Stonings were presumably the standard form of judicial execution in biblical times.

Why was Stephen stoned to death? Jews did not kil Jesus by stoning to death; instead they presented Jesus before Pilate, as an offender who, according to them, deserved death penalty. The same crowd, who was reluctant to stone Jesus to death by stoning, resorted to killing Stephen by stoning to death, illegally.

Almighty Father sent His only Son into this world at a very appropriate time during the regime of Roman Government. As Paul puts it…

"For when we were yet without strength, in due time Christ died for the ungodly". (Romans 5:6)

"Who gave himself a ransom for all, to be testified in due time" (1 Timothy 2:6)

It was a time when Roman Government was in power and the age old punishment of 'stoning to death' was abolished. Jews had no power to execute 'capital punishment', but to seek authority from the erstwhile Government to execute Jesus to death.

The only recourse for them to avoid public revolt against them, and of getting blamed of taking the law into their hands. They took Jesus to Pilate to render a judgment on Jesus.

All the while before they brought Jesus before Pilate, they were accusing the Lord of 'blasphemy', but suddenly they changed their allegations against Him to three points which, they thought, were punishable by death on the cross. John Chapter 8 has the details as to how they mocked Jesus as the son of Mary and Joseph and a son of carpenter. They ridiculed Him when He said He was before Abraham, and that He came from heaven.

They alleged Jesus of insurrection against Government

They alleged Jesus of not paying taxes

They alleged Jesus of calling Himself a King

All the three charges stood no ground. Jesus never resorted to insurrection against Government.

Jesus always did good for the people. He gave sight to the blind, He healed those who were possessed by demons. He healed the sick, and not a single time He did anything against the Government. He said render unto Caesar that which belongs to Caesar and render unto God that which belongs to God.

Jesus paid taxes by extracting coin from the mouth of the fish.

Jesus said this world does not belong to Him, and He will come again in glory.

In all these three charges Jesus was proved innocent, and yet the voice of the people prevailed when they cried "crucify him, crucify him".

Pilate, unjustly handed Jesus over to Jews for crucifixion on the cross. On the Cross, yes! That was the punishment for criminals during that period of time.

Lord Jesus was crucified between two criminals, as if to show that Jesus was a similar criminal as those two criminals were, even though he was declared 'innocent' of all the charges.

Paul writes about Jesus...

"And being found in fashion as a man, he humbled himself, and became obedient unto death, even the death of the cross" (Philippians 2:8)

It was a prophecy fulfilled, as we read...

"Christ hath redeemed us from the curse of the law, being made a curse for us: for it is written, Cursed is every one that hangeth on a tree" (Galatians 3:13)

"And if a man have committed a sin worthy of death, and he be to be put to death, and thou hang him on a tree: His body shall not remain all night upon the tree, but thou shalt in any wise bury him that day; (for he that is hanged is accursed of God;) that thy land be not defiled, which the LORD thy God giveth thee for an inheritance" (Deuteronomy 21:22-23)

"For he hath made him to be sin for us, who knew no sin; that we might be made the righteousness of God in him" (2 Corinthians 5:21)

Jews often called cross as a "tree" as it is written in Acts 5:30

Peter and other apostles said...

"The God of our fathers raised up Jesus, whom ye slew and hanged on a tree" (Acts 5:30)

"And when they had fulfilled all that was written of him, they took him down from the tree, and laid him in a sepulchre" (Acts 13:29)

Who can fathom the wisdom of the Almighty God? Right in the first book of the Bible, in Genesis 3:15 there is prophesy about the death of Jesus. It says…

"And I will put enmity between thee and the woman, and between thy seed and her seed; it shall bruise thy head, and thou shalt bruise his heel" (Genesis 3:15)

Lord Jesus defeated Satan at the cross, and the seed of the serpent bruised His heel at the cross. The death of Jesus paved the way for salvation of mankind, while the acts of Satan ended in defeat for itself.

Pharisees, Sadducees, jealous high priests collectively conspired to put Jesus to death on the cross. The punishment that an offender of Mosain Law was to be stoned to death, but Roman Government seized such power from them.

If only Jesus came into this world before the Roman Government was in power, probably Jews would have put Jesus to death by stoning. How wonderful are the works of the Almighty God that prophecies were fulfilled and Jesus was crucified on the cross.

Another reason was that Jewish leaders and Roman Government had no idea that they were ignorantly fulfilling God's plans and prophecies. Pilate asked question and the people replied as we read in Matthew 27:22)

"Pilate said unto them, What shall I do then with Jesus who is called Christ? They all said unto him, Let him be crucified" (Matthew 27:22)

Paul speaks of this mystery in 1 Corinthians 2:7,8

"But we speak the wisdom of God in a mystery, even the hidden wisdom, which God ordained before the world unto our glory: Which none of the princes of this world knew: for had they known it, they would not have crucified the Lord of glory" (1 Corinthians 2:7-8)

The worldly wisdom is seen in John 11:47-52 when the chief priests and the Pharisees gathered and said to themselves in the council, "...What are we to do?" They feared Roman Government.

"...What are we to do? For this man performs many signs. If we let him go on like this, everyone will believe in him, and the Romans will come and take away both our place and our nation." But one of them, Caiaphas, who was high priest that year, said to them, "You know nothing at all. Nor do you understand that it is better for you that one man should die for the people, not that the whole nation should perish." He did not say this of his own accord, but being high priest that year he prophesied that Jesus would die for the nation, and not for the nation only, but also to gather into one the children of God who are scattered abroad. So from that day on they made plans to put him to death" (cf. John 11:47-52 ESV)

"Now the chief priests and the Pharisees had given orders that if anyone knew where he was, he should let them know, so that they might arrest him" John 11:57

"Pilate therefore said unto them, Take him yourselves, and judge him according to your law. The Jews said unto him, It is not lawful for us to put any man to death" John 18:11

"They cried out, l"Away with him, away with him, crucify him!" Pilate said to them, "Shall I crucify your King?" The chief priests answered, "We have no king but Caesar." " John 19:15

That is why Paul said...

"For the preaching of the cross is to them that perish foolishness; but unto us which are saved it is the power of God" (1 Corinthians 1:18)"

The things that have happened during the time of Jesus were not fables, or myths, but they are historical facts, which even Historian Josephus corroborated.

"For it is written, I will destroy the wisdom of the wise, and will bring to nothing the understanding of the prudent. Where is the wise? where is the scribe? where is the disputer of this world? has not God made foolish the wisdom of this world? For since in the wisdom of God the world by wisdom knew not God, it pleased God by the foolishness of preaching to save them that believe. For the Jews require a sign, and the Greeks seek after wisdom" (1 Corinthians 1:19-22)

It was prophecy from Isaiah 29:14

"Therefore, behold, I will proceed to do a marvellous work among this people, even a marvellous work and a wonder: for the wisdom of their wise men shall perish, and the understanding of their prudent men shall be hid" (Isaiah 29:14)

"That if you shall confess with your mouth the Lord Jesus, and shall believe in your heart that God has raised him from the dead, you shall be saved. For with the heart man believes unto righteousness; and with the mouth confession is made unto salvation" (Romans 10:9-10)

☐

CHAPTER 12

PAUL PERSUADES

PHILOSOPHERS

"And also some of the Epicurean and Stoic philosophers were conversing with him. Some were saying, "What would this idle babbler wish to say?" Others, "He seems to be a proclaimer of strange deities,"—because he was preaching Jesus and the resurrection" Acts 17:18

Apostle Paul, having visited the synagogue in Thessalonica, and another at Berea goes to Athens, as a consequence aftermath violent aftermath events once at Thessalonica, and another at Berea leaves for Athens at the behest of brethren, who saw danger to him at both the cities.

In the first instance local brethren sent Paul and Silas away by night to Berea, and in the next local brethren sent him as far as the sea and Silas and Timothy remained at Berea.

The brethren, who escorted Paul out of Berea went until he reached Athens, and went back to Berea with a command from Paul that Silas and Timothy should join him at Athens.

While Paul was waiting for Silas and Timothy to join him at Athens for the ministry, his spirit was provoked within him, when he saw the city full of idols.

He discussed with Jews and the God-fearing Gentiles in the Synagogue and in the market place every day. There he also had opportunity to persuade Epicureans

(Philosophers, who were descendants of the followers of "Epicurus", and Philosophers, who were descendants of "Zeno of Citium"). He did not insult them for their beliefs, but persuaded them to know the truth.

CHAPTER 13

EPICUREANISM

Epicureanism is a Greek Philosophy founded by Epicurus. It teaches that man's aim in life is to attain absolute pleasure and peace, devoid of mental, or emotional, or stress, or need.

People have gone to the extent of interpreting this philosophy as to lead licentious, and promiscuous life. Epicureans taught that while gods exist they do not interfere in the indulgence of man's endeavors for pleasure.

Epicureans reject immortality and they believe that human beings have soul but it is mortal and material similar to that of body. They believe and teach that there is neither after-life for man nor is there any judgment for any actions he takes to attain pleasure and peace. It teaches that man should not worry for anything in life.

Fundamentally, their idea of life is to have enough food, a comfortable life, good friends, and good relations with everyone.

They believe that at death not only body perishes but soul and spirit also perish similar to that of body. Their doctrine is known as Epicurean Epitaph, which its followers wish to have it inscribed on the tombstones.

It reads…"I was not; I was; I am not; I do not care")… What a hopeless doctrine! How practical they could be!

When Paul was speaking to Epicureans it was three hundred years past after Epicureanism was founded. It was in its original form was different.

It stressed on simple life. The philosophy said the more possessions one has the more one has to worry. Gradually it was changed to attaining of pleasures of great measure crossing the boundaries of morality.

Epicureanism eventually resulted in "Pantheism", which is to worship everything and anything. It is a doctrine that says God is there in every creation, like sun, moon, trees, flowers, animals etc.

It regards the universe as a manifestation of the glory of God, and therefore, they all deserve worship. Bible on the other hand does not permit worshipping any creation, but demands that man should worship only the creator and not the creation. Evert knee shall bow in worship to Him and Him alone.

If one does not bow down to Him now, when there is opportune time, there will come soon, a time when the same one, and all others who had taken rebellious posture, will be made to bow down to Him forcibly and confess that Jesus Christ is the Lord of all! But it will be too late to repent then.

They would have lost all the opportunities given to them by then, to repent. Such of those, who do not repent now, will miss to find their names in the "Book of Life".

The Bible says all those, whose names are not found in the Book of Life, while they are being judged at the Great White Throne, will be cast into the lake of fire, where gnashing of teeth does not stop, and thirst will never quench.

Bible gives great hope to the believers in Lord Jesus Christ as Savior, who died on the cross as a substitution for us. He offered Himself as sacrifice in order that we, in our after-life be in our glorious resurrected bodies with Him forever and ever.

There is everlasting life in heaven, where there is neither pain, nor suffering, or death. Bible teaches not to worry and teaching focuses on trusting God for everything (cf. Matthew 6:25 and 1 Peter 5:7).

Bible does not teach that while gods exist they do not interfere in man's attempts to attain absolute pleasure. God interferes in our lives.

There is after-life for everyone. There is judge and the judgment after-life. Everyone has to give account of all his actions while on the earth.

"Do you not know that you are a temple of God and that the Spirit of God dwells in you? If any man destroys the temple of God, God will destroy him, for the temple of God is holy, and that is what you are" (Corinthians 3:16, 17 NASB)

"Do you not know that your bodies are members of Christ? Shall I then take away the members of Christ and make them members of a prostitute? May it never be! Or do you not know that the one who joins himself to a prostitute is one body with her? For He says, "THE TWO SHALL BECOME ONE FLESH." But the one who joins himself to the Lord is one spirit with Him.

Flee immorality. Every other sin that a man commits is outside the body, but the immoral man sins against his own body. Or do you not know that your body is a temple of the Holy Spirit who is in you, whom you have from

God, and that you are not your own? For you have been bought with a price: therefore glorify God in your body" 1 Corinthians 6:15-20 NASB)

☐

CHAPTER 14

STOICISM

Stoicism is philosophy of national character, or culture prevalent in ancient Greece. It was greatly influenced by certain teachings of Socrates. This philosophy basically deals with personal ethics.

It teaches that the path for human beings to achieve utmost happiness is found in allowing ourselves to live in the present moment as it presents itself, rather than allowing any aspect either of past life or of future to influence our decisions, and desires for pleasure or pain. Stoicism emphasizes on rejecting pleasure. It is in stark contrast of Epicureanism.

The stoics taught that human beings should develop a behavior that depicts high moral standards. Their philosophy says health, wealth, pleasure and/or pain are neither good nor bad in themselves but they form the basis on which human beings can build their behavior to depict high moral values. According to them it is not important what is said, but it is important as to how human beings behaved.

Stoics believed in developing virtue and in order to develop virtue man needs to get rid of getting emotional. One is not supposed to feel any pain or have any feelings for pleasure or joy. This philosophy leads one to develop negative attitudes, and also leads to becoming an atheist. They have no hope of eternal life.

Bible says all have sinned and come short of the glory of God.

"For the wages of sin is death; but the gift of God is eternal life through Jesus Christ our Lord" (Romans 6:23)

The wages of sin is death, but Bible does not say life of a believer in Christ is a bed of roses and/or with great pleasures, nor does it teaches that man should pursue pleasure.

Lord Jesus Christ is our rock of refuge. No one can attain absolute pleasure on this earth nor can tolerate immense pain.

No one can save oneself from damnation unless one is forgiven of one's sins and confess that Jesus is Lord and believe in heart that God raised Him from the dead on the third day. It is surely good to do good works, but doing good works for the purpose of receiving salvation is next to impossible.

It is only by grace through faith that any sinner can be saved and enter Kingdom of God.

Salvation is neither by living an ascetic life (characterized by or suggesting the practice of severe self-discipline and abstention from all forms of indulgence, typically for religious reasons), nor by climbing a thousand steps and worship god there!

Lord Jesus Christ prayed for His disciples this way…

" "I have given them Your word; and the world has hated them, because they are not of the world, even as I am not of the world. "I do not ask You to take them out of the world, but to keep them from the evil one. "They are not of the world, even as I am not of the world. "Sanctify them in the truth; Your word is truth. "As You sent Me into the world, I also have sent them into the world" (John 17: 14-18 NASB)

"Jesus answered and said unto him, Verily, verily, I say unto thee, except a man be born again, he cannot see the kingdom of God. Nicodemus saith unto him, how can a man be born when he is old? Can he enter the second time into his mother's womb, and be born? Jesus answered, Verily, verily, I say unto thee, except a man be born of water and of the Spirit, he cannot enter into the kingdom of God. That which is born of the flesh is flesh; and that which is born of the Spirit is spirit. (John 3:3-6)

CHAPTER 15

WHO KILLED JESUS: JEWS OR ROMANS?

Very often many Christians hold Jews responsible for killing Jesus; but is it true? Almost every time they speak about the death of Jesus they remind that Jews killed Jesus. It is because of either lack of Scriptural knowledge or because they hold anti-Semitic views that they spare others from the responsibility of killing Jesus. Proper examination of Scriptures reveal that it was the collective responsibility of Jews, Romans, and the people of Israel.

The conspiracy of killing Jesus originated from the Jews, and Romans and the people of Israel participated in the conspiracy. It was Roman method of execution. Jesus was crucified according to their method of execution. Roman Governor delivered Jesus unto death, and Roman soldiers drove the nails through the palms and feet of Jesus. Therefore, neither Jews nor people of Israel, or Roman Government was exclusively responsible; but they were all equally responsible for the death of Jesus Christ.

The Chief priests, the scribes, the elders of the people assembled at the palace of the high priest Caiaphas, and consulted that they might arrest Jesus by subtlety and kill him (cf. Matthew 26:3-4)

Jewish leadership demanded Roman Government to crucify Jesus even though He was declared innocent of all the charges they levied against Him. Pilate, who declared

Jesus innocent, asked Jewish leadership as to what he should to with Jesus. Of course, unless it was in the will of the Father in heaven, Pilate could not have decreed Jesus to death. Yet, Pilate was the authority in his region. He had the authority to release Jesus from being crucified. Instead, Pilate yielded to the cry of people of Israel who shouted "crucify him, crucify him"

Pilate placed before Jews and people of Israel, an offer of releasing either a noted criminal Barabbas, or Jesus. Surprisingly, the people of Israel (Jews and Gentiles collectively) expressed their desire of having Barabbas a noted criminal released, instead of Jesus.

"But the chief priests and elders persuaded the multitude that they should ask Barabbas, and destroy Jesus". (Matthew 27:20)

The people of Israel shouted the more saying "Let him be crucified"

"And the governor said, why, what evil hath he done? But they cried out the more, saying, Let him be crucified" (Matthew 27:23).

Pilate the governor, instead of taking a firm decision based on the declaration he made that Jesus is innocent of all the charges and did not deserve death penalty, washed his hands and said "I am innocent of the blood of this just person…" Then all the people answered and said "His blood be on us, and on our children.

What a curse they called upon themselves, and the curse came upon them severely when Titus in AD 70 leveled whole of Israel including Jerusalem to the ground.

The chief Priests, the high priest and Pharisees and the scribes could not tolerate the miracles and wonders done by Lord Jesus inasmuch as the works of Lord Jesus posed a severely challenge to their authority in the region. They witnessed how Jesus raised Lazarus from death, and said to themselves…

"Therefore the chief priests and the Pharisees convened a council, and were saying, "What are we doing? For this man is performing many signs. If we let Him go on like this, all men will believe in Him, and the Romans will come and take away both our place and our nation." But one of them, Caiaphas, who was high priest that year, said to them, "You know nothing at all, nor do you take into account that it is expedient for you that one man die for the people, and that the whole nation not perish." " (John 11:47-50 NASB)

"So from that day on they planned together to kill Him" (John 11:53 NASB)

They couldn't continue to allow Jesus to work signs and wonders because it threatened their position and place in the religious society they dominated.

Above all, crucifixion of Jesus was in the plan of God Himself. The prophecy in Isaiah 53:10 says it pleased the Father to bruise His Son Jesus to die substitutionary death for our redemption from the bondage of slavery under sin. Prophet Isaiah wrote about seven hundred years before the birth of Jesus as follows:

"But the LORD was pleased

To crush Him, putting Him to grief;

If He would render Himself as a guilt offering,

He will see His offspring,

He will prolong His days,

And the good pleasure of the LORD will prosper in His hand" (Isaiah 53:10 NASB)

CHAPTER 16

GOOD FRIDAY MESSAGE

Contradictions in beliefs should point surely the errors. Either Jesus Christ was right in saying "...I am the way, the truth, and the life: no man cometh unto the Father, but by me" (John 14:6 KJV), or He was wrong in saying that He is the way, the truth and the life.

Comparison of Christianity with other religions shows that ancient practices followed to find reparations (anything paid or done to make up for a wrongdoing) were similar such as offering sacrifices to God who cannot tolerate sin. In Hinduism or in Judaism animals were sacrificed as substitutionary death on behalf of sinner.

Hinduism and Christianity teach God's commandment to lead a righteous life. Violations of God's command demands punishment. In most other religions this practice of offering sacrifices did not cease.

In Judaism sacrifices are not offered because they do not have temple now. Nor do they believe in Jesus Christ as their Savior. It is an awkward situation. So is the case with Hinduism. Many still offer sacrifices to appease enraged God, who would punish the sinners.

However, there is a beautiful culmination found in Christianity that there is a Savior, who came down in the form of a servant and in the likeness of man, and offered Himself as a substitutionary sacrifice. Lord Jesus died on behalf os sinners.

The only need for a sinner to be reconciled to God and everlasting life, is to accept the fact that Jesus died on the cross for our sake, and accept Him as Lord, and believe in hear that God raised Him from the dead on the third day from the dead. (cf. Romans 10:9-10)

The fundamental difference is that Christianity teaches that penalty for our sin has already been paid for by the substitutionary death of Jesus Christ on the cross. It is hard truth that either one has to keep offering sacrifices as reparations time and again until death, and yet have no salvation, or have your sins forgiven once and for all by believing in Lord Jesus Christ.

CHAPTER 17

WHAT BENEFIT IT IS OF IF WE DO NOT KNOW WHAT WE BELIVE IN

As I wrote earlier no offence is meant to any individual or any religion. This write up is an attempt to gain knowledge and not to offend anyone. I have many Hindu friends, who lived excellent life, with good culture, and excellent family values. Therefore, I reiterate that my friends remain as my friends, even though we might differ in religious adherences, and beliefs.

For long I was under the impression that Hindus have a set of beliefs just as Christians do, or some other religions do have, but since few years now, I came to know that Hindu beliefs are conglomeration of several beliefs. What I mean is that it is a mix-up of several spiritual traditions dating back even beyond Indus Valley Civilization.

It is purely a regional religion within the confines of India and Indian Subcontinent, as I understand. However, it is recognized in many countries based on the fact that many Indians live all over the world.

It is with regret I have to say that majority of Hindus do not know the origin of Hinduism, and what exactly they believe in. Many, who try to explain, would do so, with many flawed assertions.

Some start with Indus Valley Civilization and say, without any proof, or record that the fundamentals of Hindu beliefs were taught by the Aryans, who invaded India and settled on the banks of Indus river.

Many others say that the principles of Hinduism were taught by many groups, who lived alongside the Indus River. It seems to many that the beliefs were formed based on the natural results that happen by wrong doing.

One Doctor, who was my classmate, once said that parents taught children that a goddess will get angry and damage eyes if one handles dirty cloth,.

It may be by handling dirty cloth and rubbing fingers on eyes that eyes get affected, but by attaching divine curse that goddess will get angry, they created fear and avoided their children handling dirty cloth.

The term "Hinduism" came into be known as such when a set of beliefs were observed in the seventh century B.C.

Three identifiable periods of Hinduism were from (1) 3000 BC -1200 BC (2) 1200 BC -600 BC, (3)

600 BC - until now

First, Indus Valley Civilization in North India and Vedic period

Second, Period when Upanishads came into existence.

Third, Puranas were written with concepts of Hindu Trinity of gods, namely "Brahma", "Vishnu", and "Shiva" who had female forms of Davies.

It is followed by the emergence of Buddhism, Jainism, Artha Shastra, and writing of "Bhagavad-Gita". Many others followed like Manava Dharma Shastra, Ramayana etc.

My question is what do you believe in, and what is your hope for future. Bible gives insight about Body, Soul, and Spirit.

I know Hindus believe in Soul which never dies and is eternal. It occupies another body according to the laws of "Karma". When can you expect to get "Moksha", and attain "Brahman"? (I may have had some misunderstanding. I would appreciate if my Hindu friends correct me).

It is followed by the emergence of Buddhism, Jainism, Artha Shastra, and writing of "Bhagavad-Gita". Many others followed like Manava Dharma Shastra, Ramayana etc.

My question is what do you believe in, and what is your hope for future. Bible gives insight about Body, Soul, and Spirit.

I know Hindus believe in Soul which never dies and is eternal. It occupies another body according to the laws of "Karma". When can you expect to get "Moksha", and attain "Brahman"? (I may have had some misunderstanding. I would appreciate if my Hindu friends correct me)

CHAPTER 18

THE OBVIOUS CONTAST

The following write up is for knowledge and not for dictating anyone to necessarily follow. Reader may accept or reject. No offence is meant to any religion or any person.

I am trying to post my thoughts to have a fair and open discussion with my close friends

According to 2011 Census in India Christian population is 2.78 crore that is 2.3%, which is lowest among other major religions. The following are the facts detailed in the page cited here.

https://www.indiaonlinepages.com/.../religious-population-in-...

Hindu 96.63 crore 79.8%
Muslim 17.22 crore 14.2%
Christian 2.78 crore 2.3%
Sikh 2.08 crore 1.7%
Buddhist 0.84 crore 0.7%
Jain 0.45 crore 0.4%

If we take into consideration the origins of religions in India and the increase or decrease of population of each religion, the percentage of Christian population in India is far less than the populations of Hinduism, or Muslims.

In spite of proclaiming the "obvious truth". Proclamation or sharing the Gospel of Jesus Christ was never 'more than' the criterion to match with others. I am sure Indian Constitution was never written to curtail the freedom of speech, freedom of religions

.

The roots of Hindu religion can be traced back to Vedic period, say up to 4000 years. However, if we trace back Christianity back to Jesus it is about 2000 years, and if we trace back to Judaism, from which Christianity took birth, as is evident from the Old Testament and New Testament of the Bible, and relics and "Dead Sea Scrolls". Historian Josephus's writings, it goes back to 6000 years.

We all studied Indus Valley Civilization and about Aryans and Dravidians. Hinduism is believed to have its origin in Northern India. Interactions of Aryan and Vedic cultures with Non-Ayan cultures resulted in what we call "Classical Hinduism".

The title "Christian" and "Christianity" was not given by Jesus but by the people who listened to the Gospel of Jesus Christ and thereafter it was stamped on the followers of Jesus, to insult them.. The title is intended to be derogatory .but Christians took it in their stride without offending anyone.

If we trace back to few chapters of Old Testament in Genesis we can see that Abraham was in 17th Century B.C, whose offspring from Jacob was called "Israel" and from that lineage down to David and from his lineage was born Jesus.

In spite of such rich heritage Christians are far less than the population of other religions. I wonder what should be the speed and stress that is required to match up to the numbers of other religions, and the desire of Lord Jesus Christ to preach the Gospel to make His disciples.

www.ingramcontent.com/pod-product-compliance
Lightning Source LLC
Chambersburg PA
CBHW032139040426

42449CB00005B/317